FORWARD/COMMENTARY

The National Institute of Standards and Technology (NIST) is a measurement standards laboratory, and a non-regulatory agency of the United States Department of Commerce. Its mission is to promote innovation and industrial competitiveness. Founded in 1901, as the National Bureau of Standards, NIST was formed with the mandate to provide standard weights and measures, and to serve as the national physical laboratory for the United States. With a world-class measurement and testing laboratory encompassing a wide range of areas of computer science, mathematics, statistics, and systems engineering, NIST's cybersecurity program supports its overall mission to promote U.S. innovation and industrial competitiveness by advancing measurement science, standards, and related technology through research and development in ways that enhance economic security and improve our quality of life.

The need for cybersecurity standards and best practices that address interoperability, usability and privacy has been shown to be critical for the nation. NIST's cybersecurity programs seek to enable greater development and application of practical, innovative security technologies and methodologies that enhance the country's ability to address current and future computer and information security challenges.

The cybersecurity publications produced by NIST cover a wide range of cybersecurity concepts that are carefully designed to work together to produce a holistic approach to cybersecurity primarily for government agencies and constitute the best practices used by industry. This holistic strategy to cybersecurity covers the gamut of security subjects from development of secure encryption standards for communication and storage of information while at rest to how best to recover from a cyber-attack.

Why buy a book you can download for free?   We print this so you don't have to.

Some are available only in electronic media. Some online docs are missing pages or barely legible.

We at 4th Watch Publishing are former government employees, so we know how government employees actually use the standards. When a new standard is released, an engineer prints it out, punches holes and puts it in a 3-ring binder. While this is not a big deal for a 5 or 10-page document, many NIST documents are over 100 pages and printing a large document is a time-consuming effort. So, an engineer that's paid $75 an hour is spending hours simply printing out the tools needed to do the job. That's time that could be better spent doing engineering. We publish these documents so engineers can focus on what they were hired to do – engineering. It's much more cost-effective to just order the latest version from Amazon.com

If there is a standard you would like published, let us know. Our web site is usgovpub.com

Many of our titles are available as eBooks for Kindle, iPad, Nook, remarkable, BOOX, and Sony eReaders. Buy the paperback from Amazon and get Kindle eBook FREE using MATCHBOOK. Go to https://usgovpub.com to learn more.

Why buy an eBook when you can access data on a website for free? HYPERLINKS

Yes, many books are available as a PDF, but not all PDFs are bookmarked? Do you really want to search a 6,500-page PDF document manually? Load our copy onto your Kindle, PC, iPad, Android Tablet, Nook, or iPhone (download the FREE kindle App from the APP Store) and you have an easily searchable copy. Most devices will allow you to easily navigate an ePub to any Chapter. Note that there is a distinction between a Table of Contents and "Page Navigation". Page Navigation refers to a different sort of Table of Contents. Not one appearing as a page in the book, but one that shows up on the device itself when the reader accesses the navigation feature. Readers can click on a navigation link to jump to a Chapter or Subchapter. Once there, most devices allow you to "pinch and zoom" in or out to easily read the text. (Unfortunately, downloading the free sample file at Amazon.com does not include this feature. You have to buy a copy to get that functionality, but as inexpensive as eBooks are, it's worth it.) Kindle allows you to do word search and Page Flip (temporary place holder takes you back when you want to go back and check something). Visit **USGOVPUB.COM** to learn more.

Draft NISTIR 8213

A Reference for Randomness Beacons

Format and Protocol Version 2

John Kelsey
Lu´s T. A. N. Brandão
Ren´ Peralta
Harold Booth

**National Institute of
Standards and Technology**
U.S. Department of Commerce

Draft NISTIR 8213

A Reference for Randomness Beacons
Format and Protocol Version 2

John Kelsey
Luís T. A. N. Brandão
Ren´ Peralta
Harold Booth

Computer Security Division
Information Technology Laboratory

May 2019

U.S. Department of Commerce
Wilbur L. Ross, Jr., Secretary

National Institute of Standards and Technology
Walter G. Copan, NIST Director and Undersecretary of Commerce for Standards and Technology

30 National Institute of Standards and Technology Interagency or Internal Report 8213
31 85 pages (May 2019)

32 This publication is available free of charge from:
33 https://doi.org/10.6028/NIST.IR.8213-draft

47 **Public comment period: May 06, 2019, to August 05, 2019**

48 National Institute of Standards and Technology
49 Attn: Computer Security Division, Information Technology Laboratory
50 100 Bureau Drive (Mail Stop 8930) Gaithersburg, MD 20899-8930
51 Email: beacon-nistir@nist.gov

Reports on Computer Systems Technology

The Information Technology Laboratory (ITL) at the National Institute of Standards and Technology (NIST) promotes the U.S. economy and public welfare by providing technical leadership for the Nation's measurement and standards infrastructure. ITL develops tests, test methods, reference data, proof of concept implementations, and technical analyses to advance the development and productive use of information technology. ITL's responsibilities include the development of management, administrative, technical, and physical standards and guidelines for the cost-effective security and privacy of other than national security-related information in federal information systems.

Abstract

A randomness beacon produces timed outputs of fresh public randomness. Each output, called a pulse, also includes metadata and cryptographic elements to support several security and usability features. This document specifies a reference "version 2" of a format for pulses and of a protocol for beacon operations. The main goal of the description is to serve as a baseline for the deployment of numerous interoperable beacons, including the NIST Beacon. In the proposed reference, a Beacon periodically outputs a pulse containing 512 fresh random bits, time-stamped, signed and hash-chained. For example, each pulse also pre-commits to the randomness to be released in the next pulse. The latter enables users to securely combine randomness from different beacons. The Beacon protocol also specifies the interface for users to interact with the Beacon, in order to obtain information about past pulses.

Keywords: cryptography; public randomness; beacons; hash chaining; timestamping; auditability; unpredictability.

Acknowledgments

This reference document is an output of the NIST Beacon project, which started in 2011. Ron Rivest played an important early role in motivating the creation of the project, by pointing out to NIST that a public source of randomness could be valuable for auditing voting machines. Michael Fischer was a valuable early collaborator in thinking about a theoretical framework for public randomness. Andrew Regenscheid provided valuable administrative and technical support to the project. Overall, the NIST Beacon project has motivated several outputs, by the Information Technology Laboratory (ITL) and the Physics Measurement Laboratory (PML), involving collaboration from various NIST members, including Michael Bartock, Lawrence E. Bassham, Joshua Bienfang, Peter L. Bierhorst, Thomas Gerrits, Scott C. Glancy, Michaela Iorga, Emanuel H. Knill, Paulina Kuo, Alan Migdall, Carl A. Miller, Sae Woo Nam, Andrew Rukhin, Krister Shalm, and Michael Wayne. These outputs include the deployment of a prototype NIST randomness Beacon in 2013 (version 1), the experimental validation of Bell inequalities (a loophole-free Bell test experiment) in 2015, the development in 2017 of a random-number generator based on probabilities of quantum photon detection, the upgrade of the NIST randomness Beacon implementation in 2018 (version 2). The development of the present document benefited from the context of the NIST Beacon project. In turn, we expect this reference document to advance the development of technology related to the support of public randomness for privacy and auditability applications of societal benefit.

95   **Call for Patent Claims**

96   This public review includes a call for information on essential patent claims (claims whose use would be
97   required for compliance with the guidance or requirements in this Information Technology Laboratory (ITL)
98   draft publication). Such guidance and/or requirements may be directly stated in this ITL Publication or by
99   reference to another publication. This call also includes disclosure, where known, of the existence of pending
100   U.S. or foreign patent applications relating to this ITL draft publication and of any relevant unexpired U.S. or
101   foreign patents.

102   ITL may require from the patent holder, or a party authorized to make assurances on its behalf, in written or
103   electronic form, either:

104   a) assurance in the form of a general disclaimer to the effect that such party does not hold and does not
105   currently intend holding any essential patent claim(s); or

106   b) assurance that a license to such essential patent claim(s) will be made available to applicants desiring
107   to utilize the license for the purpose of complying with the guidance or requirements in this ITL draft
108   publication either:

109   i) under reasonable terms and conditions that are demonstrably free of any unfair discrimination; or

110   ii) without compensation and under reasonable terms and conditions that are demonstrably free
111   of any unfair discrimination.

112   Such assurance shall indicate that the patent holder (or third party authorized to make assurances on its
113   behalf) will include in any documents transferring ownership of patents subject to the assurance, provisions
114   sufficient to ensure that the commitments in the assurance are binding on the transferee, and that the transferee
115   will similarly include appropriate provisions in the event of future transfers with the goal of binding each
116   successor-in-interest.

117   The assurance shall also indicate that it is intended to be binding on successors-in-interest regardless of whether
118   such provisions are included in the relevant transfer documents.

119   Such statements should be addressed to: beacon-nistir@nist.gov

120   This call for patent claims is defined in the "ITL Patent Policy — Inclusion of Patents in ITL Publications"
121   available at https://www.nist.gov/itl/publications-0/itl-patent-policy-inclusion-patents-itl-publications

122 **Executive Summary**

123 A "randomness beacon" is a timed source of public randomness. It pulsates fresh randomness
124 at expected times, making it available to the public. This can for example consist of timely
125 generating and storing random values, timestamped, signed and hash-chained, in a publicly
126 readable database. Thereafter, any external user can freely retrieve, via database queries, any
127 past pulse (and additional associated data). This document puts forward a *reference* (version
128 2) for randomness beacons, defining a *format* for pulses and a *protocol* for beacon operations.
129 The goal is to promote the development of an ecosystem of interoperable beacons. This
130 reference is labeled as "version 2" for distinction from the initial format (version 1) used by
131 the NIST Randomness Beacon prototype deployed in 2013.

132 The development of trustworthy sources of public randomness will enable applications
133 and services of societal benefit. Beacons offer the potential to improve fairness, auditability
134 and efficiency in numerous societal applications that require randomness. Examples include
135 selection of control groups for clinical trials, random assignment of court cases to judges and
136 drawing the winning numbers in public lotteries. A notable benefit of using public random-
137 ness is in enabling after-the-fact verifiability, for the purpose of public transparency. If an
138 unforgeable transcript of interactions is available, then parties not involved in a randomized
139 procedure can still later check that the used randomness was fresh at the appropriate time.
140 Another benefit is the reduction of interaction complexity in multi-party protocols.

141 As an example, suppose that a quality-control audit requires testing items randomly
142 sampled from a set. If this procedure is in place to test potential falsification of products, then
143 it is essential that the sample be unpredictable. Otherwise, a malicious producer that would
144 be able to predict the sample would also be able to pass the test while falsifying in advance all
145 non-sampled items. There would also be problems if a malicious auditor could undetectably
146 control the sample outcome. Such auditor could then, while claiming having sampled
147 uniformly at random, bias the process into either detecting too few or too many faulty items
148 (if having help from an insider). In general, many processes involving random sampling can
149 be made more robust, trustworthy and verifiable by using a public source of randomness.

150 The present reference proposes a randomness Beacon that outputs at predictable mo-
151 ments in time a pulse containing 512 unpredictable bits of fresh randomness. The usefulness
152 of those pulses is enhanced by a number of auxiliary features. An important one is the
153 hash-chaining structure that ensures that a sequence of pulses constitutes an immutable
154 history. Specifically, a cryptographic hash of each pulse is bound to the next pulse by means
155 of an unforgeable digital signature. This means that for each pulse there is a single sequence
156 of previous pulses that the beacon database is able to reveal as consistent past history. Since
157 the signature is based on public-key cryptography, even an off-line party can verify and
158 prove the authenticity of a possessed pulse or sequence thereof.

159 A recurring guiding question in the development of the present reference has been: to
160 which extent should external parties place trust on the beacon, and which properties can
161 they verify? The designed pulse format and beacon protocol facilitates several features for

162 security and envisioned applications. For example, the new design facilitates the distribution
163 of trust across beacons. The idea is to allow users to obtain trustworthy randomness by
164 securely combining the randomness from several beacons. The user can get a *good* random
165 value even if a single beacon is honest and all other beacons are malicious. For this purpose,
166 the new format adds fields that enable a beacon to cryptographically commit, in each pulse,
167 to a local random value that is only revealed in the subsequent pulse. If all beacons produce
168 their pulses at the minute mark, then they have to choose their random value before seeing the
169 respective random value of the others. This allows users to obtain a final random string with
170 security assurances similar to what would be obtained through a secure *coin-tossing* protocol.

171   Another enhancement is the use of a *skiplist* structure, allowing a more efficient veri-
172 fication of linkage between two pulses with distant timestamps. In a simple hash chain, such
173 verification required analyzing all intermediate pulses, e.g., more than two million pulses
174 between 2013 and 2018. In the new structure (version 2) fewer than 200 pulses are sufficient
175 to check the linkage between any two pulses originated with a time separation of 50 years.

176   The new format also provisions, by means of a uniform resource identifier (URI) field,
177 the original source of pulses and the identification of the Beacon authority. This is aligned
178 with another goal of this document — to promote that several beacons co-exist as separate
179 administrative identities, including across different countries. An essential goal of this
180 document is to promote interoperability across beacons. For example, the timestamp of
181 pulses is now encoded (up to milliseconds precision) in Universal Time Coordinated (UTC)
182 format, to facilitate comparison of timestamps independently of local timezones.

183   Applications of a public randomness require a number of security and cryptographic
184 guarantees. For better trustworthiness, a main challenge is enhancing security against insider
185 threats. For example, it is important to mitigate the possibility of pre-calculation of an un-
186 bounded number of pulses by a malicious beacon operator. Version 2 provides a new layer of
187 prevention against this, by provisioning in the new pulse format the insertion of unpredictable
188 external values. Scheduling such insertions technically prevents, before each external value
189 is known, advance calculation of pulses with timestamps beyond the time of insertion.

190   Other security aspects are not externally verifiable but warrant appropriate care. For
191 example, the internal clock must be well synchronized with global UTC time to ensure timely
192 generation and release of calculated randomness. As another example, the pulse randomness
193 must be obtained by a proper cryptographic combination and transformation of the output
194 of more than one random number generator (RNG). This mitigates the otherwise adverse
195 consequences that would arise from a single RNG being compromised. These operational
196 protocol aspects that are not externally verifiable are sometimes called beacon *promises*.

197   The interoperability goal also includes allowing users to interact similarly with different
198 beacons. For this purpose, this document also specifies a set of core interface rules defining
199 how external users can query the beacon database. The beacon web frontend is assumed
200 to have a interface that translates well-formed URIs into respective database queries, which
201 then elicit replies. This allows users to obtain previously generated pulses, or sequences
202 thereof, as well as system values not in pulses (e.g., public verification keys and certificates).

Table of Contents

List of Figures

List of Tables

1 Introduction

321

322 This document defines a *reference* for randomness beacons. At high level, a randomness bea-
323 con is a service that regularly outputs randomness, along with cryptographically associated
324 metadata, including timestamps and cryptographic signatures. Each output of a beacon is
325 called a *pulse*. A chronological sequence of pulses with certain semantic relations is called
326 a *chain*. Within the context of a chain in a beacon, an individual pulse can be unequivocally
327 identified by the value in some of its fields, e.g., by the timestamp (in `timeStamp`) or by
328 the pulse index (in `pulseIndex`).

329 Defining a beacon involves describing the *format* for pulses and a corresponding *protocol*
330 for beacon operations. NIST deployed in 2013 an initial beacon prototype (version 1). In
331 comparison, this document describes a *reference*, called version 2, that uses a new *format*
332 and *protocol* for randomness beacons. Interoperability advantages are expected to arise from
333 having several administratively independent beacons adhere to this new reference.

334 The *format* defines the fields in pulses and their configuration. Knowledge of the format
335 is needed by users to correctly interpret the information contained in pulses and to verify
336 their correctness. External users can verify whether or not the beacon is following the format.

337 The *protocol* consists of operational guidelines. Some relate to the secure and timely
338 *generation* of pulses by the beacon, to ensure good quality randomness output, e.g., fresh and
339 unpredictable (with full entropy). Other guidelines relate to the *timely* release of generated
340 pulses to a publicly readable database. The adherence by the beacon to some of these
341 guidelines is not externally verifiable. Some of those unverifiable protocol guidelines can
342 be called *promises*. There are also guidelines specifying the interface calls (a.k.a. queries)
343 that enable external users to perform (e.g., web based) efficient *retrieval* of past pulses (and
344 associated information).

1.1 Related work

345

346 Randomness beacons were proposed by Rabin in 1983 [Rab83], as a way to implement
347 certain cryptographic applications. In a simple version, the beacon would periodically
348 pulsate a timestamped and signed integer. Such integers could be used for contract signing
349 between several parties. For more complex applications, such as "confidential disclosures",
350 a beacon would pulsate a sequence of n random public keys and, at a latter time, would
351 reveal only one of the respective private keys.

352 Public randomness can be useful in cryptography [HL93]. Over the years, public ran-
353 domness beacons have been considered for various other cryptographic applications, e.g.,
354 traceable signatures [KTY04], voting protocols [MN10], currency mixes for anonymous
355 payments in cryptocurrencies [BNM⁻14].

356 It is often possible to replace the beacon by well-studied cryptographic primitives

357 from the areas of zero-knowledge proofs and secure multiparty computation. However, a
358 trusted randomness beacon remains useful as a facilitator of practical protocols with reduced
359 interaction between many parties, as well as of public verifiability of randomized procedures.

360 Several works have looked at providing public randomness based on decentralized
361 sources of entropy e.g., based on atmospheric noise [Haa18], financial data [CH10], crypto-
362 currencies [BCG15], and lotteries [BDF⁺15].

363 A major concern with public sources of randomness is trust. How to know if a beacon
364 is trustworthy? From a user perspective, a way to avoid trusting a single beacon is to use
365 randomness determined by different beacons. This is conceptually similar to the idea of
366 using randomness from two parties to ensure a secure coin-flipping [Blu81]. Recent works
367 have demonstrated the ability to implement systems composed of a secure combination
368 of randomness from many beacons, where some can be malicious (including aborting).
369 Examples of these systems include RandHerd and RandHound [SJK⁺17], SCRAPE [CD17],
370 and HydRand [SJSW18].

371 Version 1 of the NIST Randomness Beacon was active as an online prototype starting
372 September 05, 2013 [NIS18]. It outputted a string of 512 random bits per minute, along with
373 metadata that included a time-stamp and signature. This is conceptually close to the first
374 type of beacon described by Rabin, since it generates uniform numbers that are timestamped
375 and signed. Version 2 of the NIST Randomness Beacon uses the new format that is described
376 in this document. Pulses in the new format contain additional fields. For example, Version 2
377 pulses contain fields enabling secure coin-tossing based on randomness from various beacons.
378 Other randomness beacon projects, external to NIST, will implement beacons that are inter-
379 operable with Version 2. These include projects in Chile [CLC18] and in Brazil [INM18].

380 1.2 Recommendations and requirements

381 This document provides some guidance promoting interoperable Beacon implementations.
382 The guidance includes *recommendations* and *requirements* related to the reference for Ran-
383 domness Beacons put forward. These are sometimes expressed using terms formatted in
384 small caps and bold weight, with special meaning as follows:

385   • "SHALL" and "SHALL NOT" indicate requirements to be followed strictly in order to
386   conform to the publication and from which no deviation is permitted;

387   • "SHOULD" and "SHOULD NOT" indicate that among several possibilities one is rec-
388   ommended as particularly suitable, without mentioning or excluding others, or that a
389   certain course of action is preferred but not necessarily required, or that (in the negative
390   form) a certain possibility or course of action is discouraged but not prohibited.

391   • "MAY" and "NEED NOT" indicate a course of action permissible within the limits of
392   the publication.

393   • "CAN" and "CANNOT" indicate a possibility and capability, whether material, phys-
394   ical or causal.

1.3 Version numbering

396 This document covers the version 2 of the Beacon reference. We specify as "2.0.0" the
397 detailed version number of the current reference. Future non-major updates of this reference
398 SHOULD update the version to "2.y.z" (where y and z are non-negative integers). Those
399 potential future revisions SHOULD be defined within revisions of this NISTIR document
400 or related official documentation.

401   Incrementing z (starting at 0 for each new y) SHALL correspond to simple patches that
402 do not break any handling of previous pulses, and which do not require reinitializing any
403 ongoing chain. For example, this CAN be from assigning a new cryptographic primitive
404 to a previously non-assigned value in the cipherSuite field, by requiring support to new
405 interface calls, or by defining for the status field the meaning of previously undefined
406 bit-flags (without deprecating existing ones).

407   We say that a simple increment of z corresponds to a sub-version update, which does not
408 require being reflected within the version field of a pulse, which only show the version up
409 to the y level, i.e., "2.y" (e.g., "2.0"), omitting z.

410   Incrementing y (e.g., going from version "2.0.z" to "2.1.0") SHALL correspond to
411 changes that require distinct handling across values y. This CAN be for example from
412 adding a new field of required parsing by the signature algorithm, by changing the way an
413 existing field is calculated, or changing the handling of some previously defined bit flag in
414 the statusCode field.

1.4 Note to Reviewers

416 We seek constructive feedback from interested parties, including about the specification of
417 pulse format, cryptographic primitives, interface calls, applications, recommendations and
418 requirements, security analysis, terminology, and related-work references.

1.5 Document structure

420 The remainder of the document is organized as follows: Section 2 defines terminology and
421 notation. Section 3 overviews the beacon protocol and the pulse fields. Section 4 specifies
422 in detail all the fields of a pulse. Section 5 explains the hash-chaining of pulses and the
423 corresponding skiplists. Section 6 describes the interface that allows users to obtain past
424 pulses and associated data. Section 7 provides guidelines for using beacon randomness,
425 including how to combine randomness from several beacons. Section 8 makes a security
426 analysis. Section 9 mentions some aspects open to consideration with respect to additional
427 functionality and changes in format.

2 Terminology and notation

429 This section defines terminology and notation that will be used throughout this document.

2.1 Terminology

431 The term *Beacon* denotes the service that provides timestamped, signed and hash-chained
432 random numbers. Figure 1 illustrates, at a high level, the components of a beacon:

1. *(beacon) engine* — The internal parts of the beacon service where the actual pulses are formed. This is a computer with well-defined physical boundaries. It includes an internal clock, and internal RNG and the capabilities needed to run the "Beacon App" software. These parts are not accessible to the outside.

2. *(web) frontend* — The public-facing parts of the beacon, providing a web interface to answer requests of information stored in a database (DB). All past pulses, and certain associated data, are stored in the DB.

3. *hardware security module* (HSM) — A device independent from the beacon engine, safeguarding cryptographic keys and performing cryptographic operations.

4. *random number generator* (RNG) — A hardware-based generator of true random numbers. At least two RNGs **SHALL** be used in a randomness beacon, and at least one **SHOULD** be independent of the Beacon engine. Additional RNGs **MAY** be used.

445 The following terms relate directly to the generation of pulses:

- *pulse* — The periodic message output from a beacon, which contains a timestamp, a signature, and a random number, among other fields (described in Section 4).

- *chain* — A sequence of hash-chained pulses, produced consecutively, with a fixed chain index and increasing pulse index. All pulses in a chain follow the same format.

- *period* — The fixed time window between expected consecutive pulses in a chain. For the current NIST Beacon this is one minute (specified as 60,000 milliseconds).

- *gap* — A time interval during which one or more regularly-scheduled pulses were not produced by the beacon, presumably due to some kind of outage.

2.2 Notation for pulses and fields

455 **A pulse from a beacon and within a chain.** The symbol P is used to denote a pulse. In
456 examples hereafter, the beacon authority and the scope of a chain are often left implicit.

457 **Field names.** A pulse is composed of several fields. The expression $P.\langle fieldname \rangle$ repre-
458 sents the value in field $\langle fieldname \rangle$ of pulse P. Text in monospaced font type (teletype) is

4

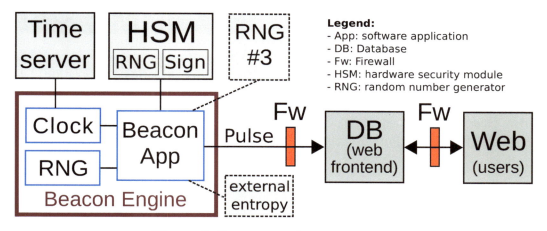

Figure 1. Beacon service components

used for concrete field names, e.g., `pulseIndex`, `timeStamp` and `localRandomValue`. For example, P.`pulseIndex` is the pulse index of pulse P.

Pulses identified by index. When the beacon authority (e.g., A) and the chain (e.g., j) are clear or implicit in the context, pulses CAN be identified via the pulse index i. For example, P_i is the ith pulse in the chain. Pulse indices are consecutive positive integers, starting with 1, implying P_i.`pulseIndex` $= i$. There are never gaps of pulse indices within the same chain, so if a pulse P_i exists for some $i \geq 2$, then P_{i-1} also exists. Since `pulseIndex` is a unique identifier of a pulse (within a chain and within a beacon domain), we CAN use $\langle fieldname \rangle_i$ (e.g., `timeStamp`$_i$) as an abbreviation to denote $P_i.\langle fieldname \rangle$.

Pulses identified by timestamp. $P[T]$ denotes the pulse P with a timestamp T, i.e., satisfying P.`timeStamp` $= T$, indicating the time promised by the Beacon to not have yet released the pulse. T does not necessarily represent the exact release time (see Section 3.3). The abbreviation $\langle fieldname \rangle[T]$ (e.g., `outputValue`$[T]$) denotes the value $P[T].\langle fieldname \rangle$.

Timestamps are represented as byte strings, using the format described in RFC3339 [NK02]. For example, 2018-07-23T19:26:00.000Z represents the time-of-day equal to 19 hours, 26 minutes, 0 seconds and 0 milliseconds in the 23rd day of July of the year 2018.

Different beacons and chains. The distinction of pulses from different beacons and/or different chains CAN be made via indices in the pulse symbol P. For example, $P_A[T]$ and $P_B[T]$ represent two pulses from beacons A and B, respectively, both associated with the same timestamp T. Several indices CAN be used concurrently, e.g., $P_{A,j,i}$ denotes the ith pulse in the jth chain of beacon A.

480 ## 3 Protocol and pulse fields

481 There are many things a beacon operator needs to do in order to provide a useful Beacon.
482 We partition the beacon-protocol guidelines into two main categories of operation:

483   1. *generation and release of pulses* — related to computation and release of pulses **by**
484   **the Beacon engine**; this part of the protocol deals with verifiable properties of the
485   format of pulses and relations between pulses (Section 3.1), as well as with externally-
486   unverifiable *promises* (Section 3.3), and other *recommendations* (Section 3.5).

487   2. *retrieval* (interface) — related to user *interface* at the web-frontend (see Section 3.6).

488   Some aspects introduced in this section are further detailed in later sections, e.g., the
489 pulse format (Section 4) and the retrieval interface (Sections 5 and 6). Certain aspects of
490 implementation security outside the scope of this section are described as an operational
491 baseline in Section 8.2.

492 ### 3.1 Pulse fields

493 The NIST Beacon pulse format 2.0 includes the following 21 fields:

494   F_1. `uri` — a uniform resource identifier (URI) that uniquely identifies the pulse;

495   F_2. `version` — the version of the beacon format being used;

496   F_3. `cipherSuite` — the ciphersuite (set of cryptographic algorithms) being used;

497   F_4. `period` — the number (denoted by π) of milliseconds between the timestamps of this
498   pulse and the expected subsequent pulse;

499   F_5. `certificateId` — the hash of the certificate that allows verifying the signature in
500   the pulse; the full certificate must be available via the website of the beacon;

501   F_6. `chainIndex` — the chain index (integer identifier, starting at 1) of the chain to which
502   the pulse belongs;

503   F_7. `pulseIndex` — the pulse index (integer identifier, starting at 1), conveying the order
504   of generation of this pulse within its chain;

505   F_8. `timeStamp` — the time (UTC) of pulse release by the Beacon Engine (the actual
506   release time **MAY** be slightly larger, but **SHALL NOT** be smaller);

507   F_9. `localRandomValue` — the `hash()` of two or more high-quality random bit sources;
508   (For all practical purposes, it is expected to have full entropy; in rigor it **MAY** forfeit
509   up to less than one bit of entropy, while indistinguishable from uniformly random.)

510   F_{10}. `external.sourceId` — the `hash()` of a text description of the source of the external
511   value, or an all-zeros byte string (with exactly $hLB = \lceil |hash()|/8 \rceil$ bytes) if there is
512   no external value;

513   F_{11}. `external.statusCode` — the status of the external value;

6

514 F_{12}. external.value — the hash() of an external value, drawn from a verifiable external
515   source from time to time, or an all-zeros string if there is no external value;

516 F_{13}. previous — the outputValue of the **previous** pulse;

517 F_{14}. hour — the outputValue of the first pulse in the (UTC) **hour** of the previous pulse;

518 F_{15}. day — the outputValue of the first pulse in the (UTC) **day** of the previous pulse;

519 F_{16}. month — the outputValue of the first pulse in the (UTC) **month** of the previous
520   pulse;

521 F_{17}. year — the outputValue of the first pulse in the (UTC) **year** of the previous pulse;

522 F_{18}. precommitmentValue — the hash() of the *next* pulse's localRandomValue;

523 F_{19}. statusCode — the status of the chain at this pulse;

524 F_{20}. signatureValue — a signature on all the above fields;

525 F_{21}. outputValue — the hash() of all the above fields.

526 **Field names, types and aliases.**   Table 1 lists all field names and their types. Field names
527 just serve a labeling purpose, not being used as input to computation (e.g., hash or signature)
528 of any pulse field. The table also defines aliases used for conciseness in this document.

Table 1. Field names, aliases and types

#	Default name	Alias	Default type		#	Default name	Alias	Default type
F_1	uri		uriStr		F_{12}	external.value	ext.value	hashOut
F_2	version		verStr		F_{13}	previous	out.Prev	hashOut
F_3	cipherSuite	cipher	uint32		F_{14}	hour	out.H	hashOut
F_4	period		uint32		F_{15}	day	out.D	hashOut
F_5	certificateId	certId	hashOut		F_{16}	month	out.M	hashOut
F_6	chainIndex	chainId	uint64		F_{17}	year	out.Y	hashOut
F_7	pulseIndex	pulseId	uint64		F_{18}	precommitmentValue	preCom	hashOut
F_8	timeStamp	time	dateStr		F_{19}	statusCode	status	uint32
F_9	localRandomValue	randLocal	hashOut		F_{20}	signatureValue	sig	sigOut
F_{10}	external.sourceId	ext.srcId	hashOut		F_{21}	outputValue	randOut	hashOut
F_{11}	external.statusCode	ext.status	uint64					

"uriStr", "verStr" and "dateStr" denote UTF8 character strings with respective structural restrictions to URI, version number and UTC date. "uint32" and "uint64" respectively denote 32-bit and 64-bit unsigned integers.

529 **Data types.**   A *pulse* is a structure composed of 21 fields, of which: eleven (11) are hash
530 outputs; one (1) is a signature output; three (3) are characters strings; three (3) are unsigned
531 integers; three (3) are bit-flag sequences or value-sets also fitting within an unsigned integer.

532   Fields have further associated structure. For example, "dateStr" is a character-string type
533 that must be specified within the UTC format and incorporates an implicit *linear order* ($\leq$)
534 that allows chronological comparison of any two timestamps.

535   The indication of default data types in Table 1 serves an informative purpose, but the
536   field values CAN be represented in various ways depending on the purpose. For example,
537   when performing serialization, "hashOut" (for hash outputs) and "sigOut" (for signature
538   output) CAN both be converted to byte string format (Byt) when used for hashing, or to
539   hexadecimal format (hex) when output within a MIME type text/plain document.

540   Section 4.1 discusses in more detail the field types and data representations.

3.2 Relations of field values within each chain

542   The pulses within each chain must satisfy formatting and relational rules (further detailed
543   along Section 4).

Constant or incremental fields.   For example, the following short identities hold:

545   • $\text{pulseId}_{i+i} = \text{pulseId}_i + 1 = i + 1$ (each new pulse increments the pulse index by 1);

546   • $\text{out.Prev}_i = \text{randOut}_{i-1}$ (the out.prev of a pulse is the randOut of the previous pulse);

547   • version, cipher, period and chainId remain constant (and because of that do not
548   require specification of the pulse index).

549   • $\text{time}_{i+1} = \text{time}_i + (1 + g_i) \times \text{period}$, where g_i is a non-negative integer (usually 0)
550   representing the number of pulse gaps immediately before pulse i (the condition $g_i > 0$
551   also has an implication on statusCode_i).

Serialization.   A rigorous description of the relation between the values of some fields
553   requires specifying how field values are serialized when used as input to a hash function.
554   We use an upper bar to denote byte serialization, i.e., $\overline{\langle \mathit{fieldname} \rangle}_i$ denotes the byte-string
555   serialization of $\langle \mathit{fieldname} \rangle_i$. If the field is not of integer type (uint32 or uint64), then
556   its serialization also includes as a prefix the field length encoded as a (serialized) 64-bit
557   unsigned integer. Section 4.1.2 describes the details of serialization.

Relations involving a hash function.   Let $\text{F}_{k,i}$ denote $P_i.\text{F}_k$, i.e., the value in the field F_k
559   in the pulse with index i. Let $||$ denote concatenation. For succinctness, we CAN write:

560   • $F_{21,i} = \text{randOut}_i = \text{hash}\left(||_{k \in \{1,\dots,20\}} \overline{\text{F}_{k,i}}\right)$, i.e., the output value (randOut_i) is the
561   hash() output of the "serialized" concatenation of encodings of all other fields.

562   • $F_{20,i} = \text{sig}_i = Sign\left(S_K, \text{hash}\left(||_{k \in \{1,\dots,19\}} \overline{\text{F}_{k,i}}\right)\right)$, where $Sign$ is the signature algorithm
563   (corresponding to the cipher value), with its first argument S_K holding the secret
564   signing key (for which there is a certificate(s) with hash equal to certId), and its
565   second argument S_K being the hash to be signed.

566   Similarly, we CAN write relations using aliases, such as:

8

567   • $\mathtt{randOut}_i = \mathtt{hash}\big(\overline{\mathtt{uri}_i}||\overline{\mathtt{version}_i}||\overline{\mathtt{cipher}_i}||\overline{\mathtt{period}_i}||\overline{\mathtt{certId}_i}||\overline{\mathtt{chainId}_i}||\overline{\mathtt{pulseId}_i}||$
$\overline{\mathtt{time}_i}||\overline{\mathtt{randLocal}_i}||\overline{\mathtt{ext.srcId}_i}||\overline{\mathtt{ext.status}_i}||\overline{\mathtt{ext.value}_i}||$
$\big(||_{x\in\{\mathtt{Prev,F,D,M,Y}\}}\overline{\mathtt{out}.x_i}\big)||\overline{\mathtt{preCom}_i}||\overline{\mathtt{status}_i}||\overline{\mathtt{sig}_i}\big)$

568   • $\mathtt{preCom}_i = \mathtt{hash}\big(\overline{\mathtt{randLocal}_{i+1}}\big)$

569 **Assembling a pulse.**   Figure 2 illustrates the generation of a pulse P_i. It depicts how to
570 combine several fields to compute $\mathtt{sig}_i$ and $\mathtt{randOut}_i$. For simplicity, the depiction omits
571 details about the serialization of fields, including about the ordering and encoding of the
572 inputs to various hashes.

573   In the Figure: $\rho_{i,j}$ is the "raw" random 512-bit string produced by the jth RNG; M_i is the
574 input (the needed serialization is left implicit) for the hash of the signature algorithm; S_i is
575 the signature output; and P_i, produced by *Pulsify*, is the ith pulse in some structure decodable
576 by the database (DB). The DB CAN later provide pulses in various formats, e.g., *bare* or
577 XML. For example, the bare format is $bare(P_i) = ||_{k\in\{1,...,21\}}\overline{F_{k,i}}$

578   The hash of M_i is represented with an asterisk (Hash*) because it is actually the hash
579 specified by the signature protocol (e.g., RSA PKCSv1.5). The hashing is not repeated
580 inside the illustrated Signing module. The reason for representing it outside of the HSM
581 (where the Signing module is) is to convey that it is possible to even prevent the HSM from
582 learning in advance the information needed to compute the "output value" ($\mathtt{randOut}$) of the
583 pulse. This is relevant for an adversarial setting where the HSM is semi-honest.

584 3.3 *Promises* generation and release

585 A beacon service SHOULD, via its frontend, make pulses available at a steady and predictable
586 rate. This requires a proper functioning of the backend, where the Beacon engine makes
587 certain *promises* on which unpredictability, freshness, timeliness and unambiguity hinge.

588   • **Promise 1: No advanced release.** The Beacon engine SHALL NOT release before
589   time T a pulse with timestamp T.

590   • **Promise 2: Generate with entropy.** The Beacon engine SHALL compute $\mathtt{randLocal}$
591   in each pulse as the $\mathtt{hash}()$ of at least two outputs from independent random number
592   generators, each expected to have as much entropy as the size of the $\mathtt{randLocal}$ field.

593   • **Promise 3: No advanced generation.** When internally computing $\mathtt{randLocal}_{i+i}$
594   needed for the calculation of $\mathtt{preCom}_i$, the Beacon engine SHALL sample the needed
595   randomness ($\rho_{i,j}$, for $j = 1,2[,...]$) from the several local RNGs only after releasing
596   the previous pulse (P_{i-1}) and after time $\mathtt{timeStamp}_i - \pi$.

597   • **Promise 4: No delayed release.** If until time $T + \pi/4$ the Beacon engine has not
598   released a pulse with timestamp T, then it SHALL avoid such release and enforce a
599   time-gap in the chain.

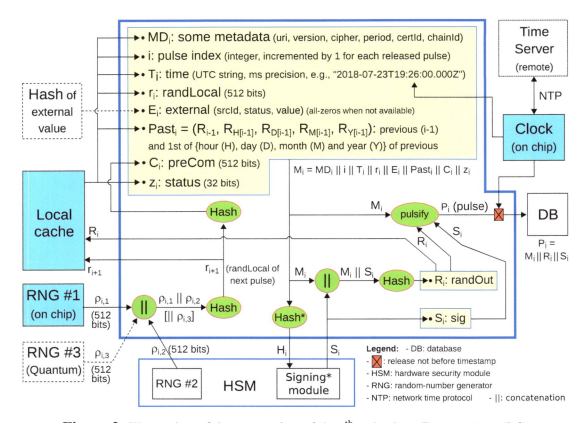

Figure 2. Illustration of the generation of the ith pulse by a Beacon App (2.0)

- **Promise 5: Unambiguous indexation.** A beacon **SHALL**, within each chain, increment by 1 the pulse index of each newly released pulse, and **SHALL NOT** release two pulses with timestamps separated by less than one period (π).

In the above *promises* the words "time" and "release" are defined from the perspective of the Beacon engine. Therefore, it is essential to ensure that the local clock of the Beacon engine is adequately synchronized with UTC.

The above requirements are called "promises" because compliance with them, even though essential for security, **CANNOT** in general be verified by outsiders. The trust that users place on the Beacon service should thus depend on the trust they can place on the upholding of these promises by the Beacon engine. The promises are subject to being broken by a crooked beacon operator, or by an outside attacker compromising the beacon engine, or by some kind of programming error or equipment failure.

In a non-compromised beacon engine, the promises imply the following properties:

- Promises 1 and 2 $\Rightarrow$ **unpredictability** of "rands": $\texttt{randOut}_i$ and $\texttt{randLocal}_{i-1}$ remain unpredictable to outsiders at least until the time instant $\texttt{timeStamp}_i$.

- Promise 3 $\Rightarrow$ **freshness**: $\texttt{randOut}_i$ and $\texttt{preCom}_i$ depend on randomness sampled

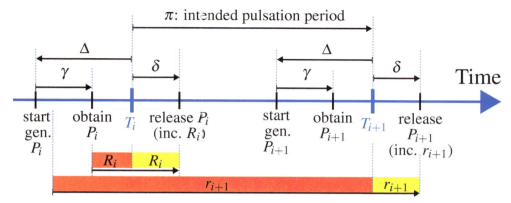

Legend:
gen. (generating); inc. (including);
γ: time taken to generate a pulse;
Δ: anticipation of generation start;

T_i: scheduled allowed time for P_i release;
δ: release delay, after allowed release time;
R_i: P_i.randOut; r_{i+1}: P_{i+1}.randLocal.

(Section 8.3.1 describes a solution that significantly reduces the window of predictability of randLocal)

Figure 3. Timeline of pulse generation and release

within less than one pulsation period from timeStamp$_i$; whenever statusCode$_i = 0$, which implies $i > 1$ and P_i not following immediately after a time-gap, randLocal$_i$ depends on randomness sampled within less than two pulsation periods from timeStamp$_i$.

- Promise 4 ⇒ **timeliness**: except in cases of time-gaps and/or of delays or failures outside the Beacon engine (e.g., in the external database and frontend), each released pulse will be available to users shortly after the time indicated in its timestamp.

- Promise 5 ⇒ **unambiguity**: within a chain, an index uniquely identifies a pulse and a timestamp uniquely identifies either a gap in the chain or a pulse.

3.4 Time variables

Figure 3 shows a timeline for pulse generation and release. It depicts: the anticipated-generation-start offset Δ, before the allowed release time; the duration γ needed for pulse generation; the pulse-release offset δ, after the allowed release time. The promises require:

$$\Delta < \pi \qquad \text{(avoid too-early generation-start)} \qquad (1)$$

$$0 \leq \delta \qquad \text{(avoid too-early release)} \qquad (2)$$

$$\max(\delta, \gamma - \Delta) < \pi/4 \qquad \text{(avoid too-late release)} \qquad (3)$$

The red bars indicate the time-intervals during which a semi-honest beacon App (i.e., passively corrupted), capable of exfiltrating internal state but otherwise following the protocol, could break the *unpredictability* property with respect to randOut (R_i) and randLocal

631 (r_i). Conversely, an honest Beacon must take all reasonable precautions to avoid early
632 disclosure of components from calculated pulses.

3.5 Additional recommendations

634 The defined promises still leave some timeline flexibility. Yet, there is envisioned utility
635 in having a Beacon engine with predictable rate. Thus, besides the defined promises, we
636 *recommend* that a Beacon engine SHOULD perform the pulse release at time 0^+, and start
637 the pulse generation (including the sampling of raw randomness from the RNGs) as late
638 as possible while obtaining the pulse by time 0^-. The symbols 0^- and 0^+ mean values as
639 close as possible to 0, respectively from below or above.

640   The time restrictions SHOULD be adjusted according to the possibility of local-clock
641 skew (σ), to still meet the promises and the above-mentioned recommendations even in
642 the presence of clock drift between consecutive synchronizations. Appendix A.1 specifies
643 recommendations to promote better timing expectations and interoperable implementations:

644   • *hard recommendations* request that the maximum skew ahead (σ^+) and behind (σ^-)
645   of UTC be estimated and enforced below one tenth of the period, and that on the basis
646   of such estimation the other parameters (Δ, δ, γ) be set in such a way that the promises
647   1, 3 and 4 are met even when taking the skew into account.

648   • *soft recommendations* ask for a fine-tuning of the time parameters such that the gener-
649   ation start and end, and the release time, are all as close as possible to the timeStamp.

650   The appendix also defines the concepts of tuning slack (η) and time accuracy (α), to help
651 quantify a kind of "distance" to an ideal implementation. Tables 13 and 14 therein exemplify
652 acceptable and unacceptable parameter sets, in terms of hard time-recommendations.

3.6 Retrieval interface

654 The beacon interface determines the ability of external users to obtain released pulses and
655 associated data. Section 6 provides further details on the retrieval interface. Some requests
656 are of mandatory support, whereas others are simply recommended but left as optional in
657 this specification. For example, the beacon frontend must:

658   • Make all previous pulses available for retrieval (see Section 6.2).

659   • Provide *skiplists* upon request (see Section 6.3). (Skiplists allow efficient verification
660   of consistency between two distant pulses, as discussed in section 5.)

661   • Provide associated data which is referenced but not included in pulses; Such associated
662   data includes public-key certificates (§6.4) and external source descriptions §6.5.

663   It is recommended, though optional, that a randomness Beacon enables retrieval of any
664 other associated data that may improve usability of the beacon. This MAY include, for
665 example, pre-images of past external values (see Section 6.5).

666 **4   The Pulse Format**

667 Version 2.0 of the pulse format has become more complex, compared to the version (1) used
668 in the initial NIST beacon prototype. Some of the new complexity intends to make operating
669 a beacon easier. Other parts intend to improve the security against a misbehaving beacon.
670 Still others intend to make it easier to securely combine outputs from different beacons.

671   This section starts by describing used data formats (§4.1), for representation of fields and
672 compositions thereof, including serialization procedures. It then describes the meaning and
673 calculation procedures for each field of a pulse. The description follows the fields ordering
674 already defined in Section 3.1, but also organizing fields by topics: administrative (§4.2),
675 indexation (§4.3), the local random value (§4.4), the external source (§4.5), past outputs
676 (§4.6), precommitment (§4.7), signature related (§4.8), and the output value (§4.9).

677 **4.1   Data formatting and representation**

678 **4.1.1   Basic data formats for fields**

679 The handling of pulses and associated data involves parsing diverse elements with various
680 syntaxes and representations. For different purposes, the same data, often contextualized
681 within a field, CAN be expressed with different representations.

682   We refer to the following basic data formats:

683 • **B64:** A base 64 encoding, allowing characters A–Z, a–z, 0–9, + and /. For example,
684   it is used to encode a PEM file (whose hash() is certId) containing the public
685   certificate(s) corresponding to the secret signature key.

686 • **bin:** A UTF8 string of zeros (0) and ones (1) expressing a sequence of bits. This is
687   useful for example to describe a sequence of bit flags. The prefix "0b" (without the
688   quotes) MAY be used to denote that what follows is a value written in binary format.
689   When the length of the variable is implicit, the representation MAY omit left zeros.

690 • **Byt:** A string of bytes (bit octets), where any byte value (0 through 255) is allowed.
691   It is used for example for encoding inputs for hashing, and is not used for textual
692   printing. Two specialized formats are uint32 and uint64, correspondingly consisting
693   of 4 and 8 bytes representing unsigned integers (in big-endian order).

694 • **dec:** A UTF8 string expressing an integer in decimal format, without padding left
695   zeros; the only allowed characters are 0, 1, ..., 9.

696 • **hex:** A UTF8 string of hexadecimal characters (0, 1, ..., 9, A, B, ..., F), with the
697   letters in upper-case. The prefix "0x" (without the quotes) MAY be used to denote
698   that what follows is a value written in hexadecimal. When the length is implicit, the
699   representation MAY omit left zeros.

13

700   • **str:** A UTF8 character string [Yer03].

701 **Examples of varying representations.**

702   • randOut is a byte string when used as a hash input, but is expressed in hexadecimal
703   when part of an XML output.

704   • pulseId is an octet of bytes when used as a hash input, but is expressed as a decimal
705   string when used as a component of the uri field.

706   • status is a quartet of bytes when used as a hash input, but **CAN** also be interpreted
707   as a sequence of 32 bit-flags when describing its meaning, and **CAN** be expressed in
708   hexadecimal within some pulse representations.

709   It is thus useful to have notation to disambiguate the representation required of a field.

710 **Encoding into a basic format.**   Sometimes it is necessary to ensure that a variable is
711 converted/encoded into a particular format. Function encode is used for that purpose:

712   • encode($var, form$) denotes a value var represented in format $form$, using the minimal
713   number of base elements of format $form$.

714   • encode($var, form : len$) is the same but conditioned to an exact length len (the number
715   of base elements of format $form$), e.g., if-need-be adding leading zeros.

716   The actual transformation **MAY** depend on the format of the input, but we leave that
717 implicit. For example: when converting from hex to Byt, each pair of hexadecimal characters
718 is converted into one byte; when converting from bin to Byt, then each octet of bits is
719 converted into one byte.

720 **Endianness.**   All encodings are in big-endian order. For example:

721   • encode(x, uint32) = encode($x, Byt, 4$), receiving as input an unsigned integer x
722   between 0 and $2^{32} - 1$, encodes it as a 32-bit string in big-endian, using 4 bytes.

723   • encode(x, uint64) = encode($x, Byt, 8$), receiving as input an unsigned integer x
724   between 0 and $2^{64} - 1$, encodes it as a 64-bit string in big-endian, using 8 bytes.

725 **Examples.**

726   • encode(S, Byt) converts the input S into a sequence of bytes;

727   • encode($H, Byt : BLenHash$) converts H into a sequence of exactly $BLenHash$ bytes;

728   • ZeroH = encode($0, Byt : BLenHash$) is a constant sequence of $BLenHash$ bytes, all
729   with value 0, where $BLenHash$ is the number of bytes in a hash output.

730   • encode(S, *hex*) converts the input S into a sequence of hexadecimal characters (e.g.,
731   useful when representing hash outputs in a Txt pulse format for human readability).

732 **Alternative notation.**   It is sometimes useful to define variable strings with resort to
733 variable components/fields. The uri field is one such case, where some of its components
734 vary across pulses. In that setting, when expressing a variable supposed to be instantiated
735 with a particular format, we use the following notation:

736   • ⟨*field*:form⟩ denotes a field "field" to be replaced with a value with format "form"

737   • ⟨*field*:form:len⟩ denotes the same but conditioned to using exactly *len* base elements
738   of format "form".

4.1.2 Byte serialization of fields

740 For unambiguous transmission or processing it is sometimes useful to encode a sequence of
741 fields into a single data packet that enables proper parsing. For example, hash functions and
742 signature algorithms process inputs received as strings of bytes. Thus, when preparing the
743 input needed to compute the hashes and signature needed within a pulse, we construct the
744 corresponding byte-string input from the needed fields.

745   The process of producing a single byte-sequence from a sequence of fields is denoted
746 byte serialization (or simply *serialization*). The procedure processes each field at a time,
747 in one or two steps. If the field is of uint32 or uint64 type, then the field serialization
748 is simply the (big endian) byte encoding into 4 or 8 bytes, respectively. For other types
749 (non-integer), the field serialization produces a concatenation of two components: the second
750 component is the byte-string encoding of the field value (sometimes with a fixed length);
751 the first component is the byte-string encoding of the length (number of bytes) of the second
752 component. Table 2 shows the length after byte serialization of each default data type
753 previously identified in Table 1.

Table 2. Length after byte serialization, per default field type

Default field type	Length prepended? (8 bytes)	Number of bytes (not counting the prepended length encoding)	
		General	Example
uriStr	Yes	variable (> 33)	50 if domain=beacon.nist.gov, pulseId:dec=1 and chainId:dec=1
verStr	Yes	≥ 3	3 if version:dec="2.0"
dateStr	Yes	24	
hashOut	Yes	*BLenHash*	64 if cipher=0
sigOut	Yes	*BLenSig*	512 if cipher=0 and the RSA modulus has 4096 bits
uint32	No	4	
uint64	No	8	

15

754 **Auxiliary BytLen function.** Let $\texttt{BytLen}(S)$ return the uint64 (8-bytes) encoding of the
755 length (*len*), in number of bytes, of the byte encoding of the input S, i.e.:

$$\texttt{BytLen}(S) = \texttt{encode}(len(\texttt{encode}(S, Byt)), \texttt{uint64}). \qquad (4)$$

756 **Byte serialization of single fields.** We define three byte-serialization functions for indi-
757 vidual fields. Despite some redundancy, their distinction enable us to make more evident
758 what is the default type of each input field, and corresponding restrictions (e.g., hashes have
759 an expected fixed length).

760 • $\texttt{Byt\_serialize\_string}(S)$, receiving as input a UTF8 string, outputs a byte string,
761 resulting from the concatenation of two components: the 2nd is the byte encoding of
762 the UTF8 string S; the 1st is the BytLen of the second component. The result is:

$$\texttt{BytLen}(S) \parallel \texttt{encode}(S, Byt) \qquad (5)$$

763 *Remark.* For the UTF8-string fields $\texttt{version}$ and $\texttt{time}$, The number of bytes in the
764 UTF8-string fields $\texttt{version}$ and $\texttt{time}$ is equal to the corresponding number of UTF8
765 characters, since the characters must be within the ASCII (American Standard Code
766 for Information Interchange) collection of 128 characters. Conversely, the UTF8-
767 string field $\texttt{uri}$ is allowed to include non-ASCII characters, which require more than
768 one byte. Prefixing (an encoding of) the number of bytes, rather than the number of
769 characters, eases the process of parsing a sequence of serialized fields, since the jump
770 across fields does not requiring parsing the UTF8 characters.

771 • $\texttt{Byt\_serialize\_hash}(H)$, receiving as input a hash value, calculates its byte encod-
772 ing and then prefixes its $\texttt{BytLen}$, which must correspond to *BLenHash*. The output is:

$$\texttt{encode}(BLenHash, \texttt{uint64}) \parallel \texttt{encode}(H, Byt : BLenHash). \qquad (6)$$

773 The integer *BLenHash* is a global variable denoting the number of bytes (e.g., 64
774 bytes if the hash function is SHA512) of the hash in use within a chain. We leave
775 implicit the verification that the length of the byte encoding of the input is not larger
776 than *BLenHash*. (Otherwise the case is considered as an error.)

777 When a field of type hashOut is set to "zero" to represent an absent $\texttt{hash}()$ value, the
778 serialization produces an all-zeros string of the same length (*BLenHash* bytes) as a
779 normal $\texttt{hash}()$ output. We denote such constant byte string as $\texttt{ZeroH}$.

780 • $\texttt{Byt\_serialize\_sig}(S)$, receiving as input a signature value, calculates its byte en-
781 coding and then prefixes the corresponding BytLen, which must be the encoding of

782   *BLenSig*. The output is:

$$\text{encode}(\textit{BLenSig}, \text{uint64}) \| \text{encode}(H, \textit{Byt} : \textit{BLenSig}). \tag{7}$$

783   The integer *BLenSig* is a global variable within a chain, e.g., with value 512 if the
784   signature algorithm uses RSA with a 4096-bit modulus.

Byte serialization of a sequence of fields.   The serialization of sequences of fields is
785
786   required in several cases related to pulse handling, such as for encoding:

787   • the input of the hash that is signed to produce `sig`;

788   • the hash pre-image of `randOut`;

789   • a pulse in the bare pulse format;

790   • the hash pre-image of `ext.value`.

791   Algorithm 1 describes function `Byt_serialize_fields`, which serializes a sequence
792   (vector) of fields. The algorithm sequentially processes each field, taking into account the
793   each field type. The output is a sequence of bytes.

Algorithm 1 Serialize field sequence to a byte string.

1:    **function** BYT_SERIALIZE_FIELDS(*vector*)
2:        $\langle field_1, \ldots, field_n \rangle \xleftarrow{\text{parse}} vector$
3:        $Z \leftarrow$ "" (*empty string*)
4:        **for** $i = 1, \ldots, n$ **do**
5:            $x \leftarrow value(field_i)\ t \leftarrow type(field_i)$
6:            **if** $t = \text{uint32}$ **then** $Z \leftarrow Z \| \text{encode\_uint32}(x)$
7:            **else if** $t = \text{uint64}$ **then** $Z \leftarrow Z \| \text{encode\_uint64}(x)$
8:            **else if** $t \in \{\text{uriStr}, \text{verStr}, \text{dateStr}\}$ **then** $Z \leftarrow Z \| \text{Byt\_serialize\_string}(x)$
9:            **else if** $t = \text{hashOut}$ **then** $Z \leftarrow Z \| \text{Byt\_serialize\_hash}(x)$
10:           **else if** $t = \text{sigOut}$ **then** $Z \leftarrow Z \| \text{Byt\_serialize\_sig}(x)$
11:           **else abort**
12:       **return** (Z)

Example (input for hashing needed before signing).   The procedure for producing the
794
795   cryptographic signature (`sig`) that is part of a pulse requires hashing the sequence of
796   preceding fields. Recalling the notation introduced in Sections 3.1 and 3.2, the input of such
797   hash is equal to $\|_{k \in \{1, \ldots, 19\}} \overline{F_{k,i}}$. This is the same as

$$\text{Byt\_serialize\_fields}(vector), \tag{8}$$

798 where $vector = \langle F_{k,i} : k = 1, ..., 19 \rangle$, or, more precisely, $vector = \langle$ uri, version,
799 cipher, period, certId, chainId, pulseId, time, randLocal, ext.srcId,
800 ext.status,ext.value, out.Prev, out.H, out.D, out.M, out.Y, preCom, status $\rangle$.

801   As a concrete example, Algorithm 2 shows the unrolled serialization operation.

Algorithm 2 Serialize the hash input of the sig field of a pulse

1: $Z \leftarrow$ Byt_serialize_string(uri)
2: $Z \leftarrow Z \parallel$ Byt_serialize_string(version)
3: $Z \leftarrow Z \parallel$ encode(cipherSuite, uint32)
4: $Z \leftarrow Z \parallel$ encode(period, uint32)
5: $Z \leftarrow Z \parallel$ Byt_serialize_hash(certificateId)
6: $Z \leftarrow Z \parallel$ encode(chainIndex, uint64)
7: $Z \leftarrow Z \parallel$ encode(pulseIndex, uint64)
8: $Z \leftarrow Z \parallel$ Byt_serialize_string(timeStamp)
9: $Z \leftarrow Z \parallel$ Byt_serialize_hash(localRandomValue)
10: $Z \leftarrow Z \parallel$ Byt_serialize_hash(external.sourceId)
11: $Z \leftarrow Z \parallel$ encode(external.statusCode, uint64)
12: $Z \leftarrow Z \parallel$ Byt_serialize_hash(external.value)
13: $Z \leftarrow Z \parallel$ Byt_serialize_hash(previous)
14: $Z \leftarrow Z \parallel$ Byt_serialize_hash(hour)
15: $Z \leftarrow Z \parallel$ Byt_serialize_hash(day)
16: $Z \leftarrow Z \parallel$ Byt_serialize_hash(month)
17: $Z \leftarrow Z \parallel$ Byt_serialize_hash(year)
18: $Z \leftarrow Z \parallel$ Byt_serialize_hash(precommitmentValue)
19: $Z \leftarrow Z \parallel$ encode(statusCode, uint32)
20: **return** (Z)

---

802 ### 4.1.3 The Bare Pulse Format

803 The *bare* pulse format if a byte-string pulse representation (Byt format) that concatenates
804 all byte-serialized fields of a pulse, including corresponding prefixes of the field lengths
805 for the non-integer field types. This forms an unambiguous sequence of bytes. Recalling
806 the notation introduced in Sections 3.1 and 3.2, the bare pulse is equal to:

$$bare_i = \parallel_{k \in \{1, ..., 21\}} \overline{F_{k,i}} \tag{9}$$

807   Algorithm 3 (construct_bare_pulse()) shows a corresponding pseudo-code for generation
808 of a *bare* pulse, based on the 2 example.

Algorithm 3 Unambiguously encode an entire pulse as a byte string.

1: **function** CONSTRUCT_BARE_PULSE(uri, version, period, ..., outputValue)
2:     $Z \leftarrow$ Byt_serialize_fields(uri, version, period, ..., statusCode)
3:     $Z \leftarrow Z \parallel$ Byt_serialize_sig(signatureValue)
4:     $Z \leftarrow Z \parallel$ Byt_serialize_hash(outputValue)
5:     **return** (Z)

---

809 ### 4.1.4 The Txt pulse format

810 The Txt format for pulses intends a balance between conciseness and human-readability and
811 is aimed for inclusion in MIME type text/plain documents. It has a simple logic:

812   • It starts and ends with delimiter lines of the description of a pulse;

813   • Within the delimited description, each new line identifies a field name (abbreviated),
814   the format that follows, and the respective field value, followed by a line break.

815 This design also enables a straightforward concatenation of multiple Txt pulses.

816 Figure 4 shows a concrete example. Algorithm 4 shows concise pseudo-code for function
817 Txt_Serialize, to produce a Txt serialization of a pulse. The Txt serialization of a pulse
818 CAN be expressed as Txt_Serialize(vector), where $vector = \langle (A_i, R_i, F_i) : i = 1, ..., 21 \rangle$, with
819 the field alias A_i and the representation format R_i corresponding to field F_i being determined
820 from Table 3.

Algorithm 4 Txt serialization of a pulse

Require: Input *vector* has 21 elements
Require: Elements A_i and R_i are from Table 3
1: **function** TXT_SERIALIZE(*vector*)
2:     **print** "-----BEGIN BEACON-PULSE FORMAT TXT-----\n"
3:     **for** $i = 1, ..., 21$ **do**
4:         $x \leftarrow vector_i$
5:         **print** A_i + ":" + R_i + "=\"" + encode(x, R_i) + "\"\n"
6:     **print** "-----END BEACON-PULSE FORMAT TXT-----\n"

The sequence "\n" represents a line break; the sequence "\"" represents the double quote character ".

---

997 **Hexadecimal serialization.** When producing certain output documents, e.g., MIME type
998 text/plain, fields CANNOT use the full spectrum of bytes. A useful alternative serialization
999 is based on hexadecimal characters (0...9, A...F). Each byte (value between 0 and 255)
1000 is represented in hex format, as a pair of hexadecimal characters. For example, a 512-bit
1001 hash() output is then represented with 128 hexadecimal characters. The serialization MAY
1002 omit prefixing the length if the beginning and end of the hexadecimal string is otherwise

```
953  -----BEGIN BEACON-PULSE FORMAT TXT-----
954  uri:str="https://beacon.nist.gov/beacon/2.0/chain/1/pulse/220394"
955  version:str="Version 2.0"
956  cipher:hex="00000000"
957  period:dec="60000"
958  certId:hex="5501e3d72bc42f3b96e16de4dcadcb16768e109662bd16d667d5fd9aee585af31bbdc5dd4f53592276
959  064b53dddd76c8f3604b2a41db6e09f78f82bb5d6569e7"
960  chainId:dec="1"
961  pulseId:dec="220394"
962  time:str="2018-12-26T16:07:00.000Z"
963  randLocal:hex="5FF1E44E70C019C42C77FA72D5228A2E663416D0778BFAC826F6B4757B634B076C50ED2D5A3975C
964  BAF237C211A027EDAFF3E241A885D69EAA7237E2744E6C1E2"
965  ext.srcId:hex="0000000000000000000000000000000000000000000000000000000000000000000000000000000000
966  0000000000000000000000000000000000000000000000000"
967  ext.status:hex="0000000000000000"
968  ext.value:hex="0000000000000000000000000000000000000000000000000000000000000000000000000000000000
969  0000000000000000000000000000000000000000000000000"
970  previous:hex="BA646CC4E7AE195D2C85E9D3AE9C9722B974F2134699D2493FA9E296C34995E8E471B329CB5F6323
971  5982CEE3395A749C618E61466847951D543ADC2FBAD23ECB"
972  out.H:hex="E75A5877169CC15220BCB11C8DA18159F14B880D85C5F3E9E462D010DC49BFCFE36D116D72C1D32A95A
973  E8FFD9F0B6CE20DC073ED881BA36D5EF4687DC5B12328"
974  out.D:hex="CDD24473B4427C3D3C856C66DF669444CE79D1262F94F4CC745E037AB781245A560E722514A62BEFF9A
975  BE3B72EAFDF5EAE5A43EA806F5571B05EA04B8E7B02B7"
976  out.M:hex="A9EDA202336C7DB1F05DE3BB24AAC1B54E98C9BD46CDF3D193FAE2BF4E0CD696AD6A743DFDF4DC48E59
977  85BE329652E0A74816C7B69BBAF644FF0ACA352207FFB"
978  out.Y:hex="7665F054F21B50DF62CD3E50AF8EB783E30D271B091DE051212D301E0E3D17FFCF0367DB41CFFD3C51E
979  88BDE0B0621F49EB03435BC373D5D49480941A8B3547E"
980  preCom:hex="269908B840E79BE71991FFE62CEC4EBAEB3C050E93D71248CBB3E4358445FF0858D1D2CCF899A19B86
981  1C0C11CECCF16A0859AFD68E58481D4ADB1BE61F30E419"
982  status:hex="00000000"
983  sig:hex="17943D886DA8C7C24B9244BE5BD5DF281983D28CFFC8928846BC26529309C9724F6849F039591361DAF6B
984  8DDAB6BC275CF86F448AF1800996889508D08D8AAAD19586E7A4B04FC4C97F1DA6D619EFAE2332150328C79C23BB9F
985  E6A03E8FABDFF1AD66C5A8789D28AED4D25FF0FC5E88BE366280D7516A504EFD63706641828DDBF3C7082524F36E77
986  EE9E07A9801D0C3BAD0646AA89DDDD8E2B4C0D7F8ED67664864B598E59ABF20CA8D761BB7B32B9A32698A22935D2C7
987  127952625BB5580B2847FBBC8DFEF9039C4F5ACF12877E11121D031AED58217286F8DCF291C6E315773B42FF470B1A
988  B587F787D44381F6E655DB903F1601B65AAC86BC2B7083AEEA9B3A27A5A208674056EFBB3C44629F333C810ADAD00E
989  4FCFCE48E54F8FB7FC700598EA3E6497821736D24E5DA801A8B9DEC28A2B68E50FE13752270EB9CA7912B21EB6C104
990  E78D105D0C0A635686B9A8CA26F87A1E63F0E411FD228F21B08BCD24660B305A4A42A9229154DE364FAB4DFF257A59
991  DEA814034BF65C38A4C7AAEE79FEE5CC69010B1FE9759E23F192E218A19D9B8E95F6DD37D5D2F672E6CF0A0D457D9C
992  619B1808274C2B0B2D3A3A7A8D8B1BB423FDDC56110784F2E0B7A23F065B56EC6E40234786DAB8C840E47811950331
993  CBCFADEAD2EEE901D1C0A3A7E18D18A93089FC4E1CEFBA7571D2E47F10893D24BAD967FCA9DAEA67AD6B7F390AFC0"
994  randOut:hex="0A8863E03E200F694CBA50F0F9A009B078555FE637B07CA2C0A0E4D564080173787B26376C4762377
995  A139D1BCAA916A10419504850EB7CF91552A17FDCAA0463"
996  -----END BEACON-PULSE FORMAT TXT-----
```

Note: the value "Version 2.0" was indeed used in the version field of the exemplified pulse, but a correct implementation SHALL use "2.0" instead. The NIST beacon will correct this for pulses with chainId ≥ 2.

Figure 4. Pulse example in format Txt

1003 patent. This is the case whenever the representation is delimited by non-hexadecimal
1004 characters, e.g., double quotes as in "08A0". The prefix 0x MAY also be used to make more
1005 explicit the start of an hexadecimal string, e.g., as in "0x08A0".

1006 As another example, a pulse MAY be represented in text format, representing the se-

Table 3. Field names, formats and values for Txt Serialization

# (i)	Alias (A_i)	Format (R_i)	Value (F_i)	# (i)	Alias (A_i)	Format (R_i)	Value (F_i)	# (i)	Alias (A_i)	Format (R_i)	Value (F_i)
1	uri	str	F_1	8	time	str	F_8	15	out.D	hex:*HL*	F_{15}
2	version	str	F_2	9	randLocal	hex:*HL*	F_9	16	out.M	hex:*HL*	F_{16}
3	cipher	hex:8	F_3	10	ext.srcId	hex:*HL*	F_{10}	17	out.Y	hex:*HL*	F_{17}
4	period	hex:8	F_4	11	ext.status	hex:16	F_{11}	18	preCom	hex:*HL*	F_{18}
5	certId	hex:*HL*	F_5	12	ext.value	hex:*HL*	F_{12}	19	status	hex:8	F_{19}
6	chainId	dec	F_6	13	out.Prev	hex:*HL*	F_{13}	20	sig	hex:*SL*	F_{20}
7	pulseId	dec	F_7	14	out.H	hex:*HL*	F_{14}	21	randOut	hex:*HL*	F_{21}

HL and *SL* are used as abbreviations of *BLenHash* and *BLenSig*, respectively.

1007 quence of all fields in a sequence that favors human readability, including some fields
1008 represented in hexadecimal format, others in decimal, and others in UTF8 format.

1009 **4.1.5   Other structured pulse formats**

1010 The *bare* and the *txt* formats are not the only ways in which a pulse can be represented. As
1011 mentioned with further detail in Section 6.1.2, other generic standardized formats, such as
1012 HTML, JSON, XML, etc., are possible. The detailed definition of some of these formats is
1013 left outside this report, being deferred to auxiliary documents. Nonetheless, for the purpose
1014 of interoperability, it is currently defined that a Beacon **SHALL** be able to support at least
1015 the JSON format.

1016 Besides the mandatory values in a pulse, the additional structured formats **MAY** (option-
1017 ally) include auxiliary information (not part of the hash-chain), such as:

1018 • the order (1...21) of each mandatory field, as defined in Section 3.1;

1019 • timestamps (time) and pulse indices (pulseId) of the included past output values
1020 (out.Prev, out.H, out.D, out.M, out.Y);

1021 • the public key used for signature verification;

1022 • the timings (Δ, γ and δ) of pulse generation and release (in milliseconds).

1023 **4.2   Administrative fields**

1024 These fields tell the user how to interpret the rest of the pulse, and give general information
1025 about what to expect from the beacon.

1026 **4.2.1   URI**

1027 **Field name:**   uri

1028 **Default type:** uriStr (a type of byte-string)

1029 **Relations:** contains components derivable from `version`, `chainId` and `pulseId`.

1030 **Example.** The `uri` value in the first pulse of the first chain of the NIST Randomness
1031 Beacon version 2.0 is the following string:

$$\texttt{https://beacon.nist.gov/beacon/2.0/chain/1/pulse/1} \qquad (10)$$

1032 **Description:** It is a URI [BLFM05], specifying a valid URL from which the beacon
1033 pulse is expectedly available upon release. It is a variable length string structured as
1034 $\langle webPrefix{:}\mathrm{str}\rangle$/beacon/$\langle version{:}\mathrm{str}\rangle$/chain/$\langle cid{:}\mathrm{dec}\rangle$/pulse/$\langle pid{:}\mathrm{dec}\rangle$, where:

- 1035 • $\langle webPrefix{:}\mathrm{str}\rangle$ is a string $\langle scheme{:}\mathrm{str}\rangle{:}//\langle domain{:}\mathrm{str}\rangle/\langle optContext/{:}\mathrm{str}\rangle$, where:

  - 1036 – $\langle scheme{:}\mathrm{str}\rangle$ is the *scheme* component of a URI. In the current Beacon reference,
    1037 the only allowed scheme is `https` (Hyper Text Transfer Protocol Secure). Future
    1038 beacon references **MAY** allow other (secure) schemes.

  - 1039 – $\langle domain{:}\mathrm{str}\rangle$ is the expected beacon web domain; typically this will be a parent
    1040 of the domain certified in the public certificate(s) of the beacon signature key.
    1041 The current NIST beacon implementation uses `beacon.nist.gov` as its domain,
    1042 whereas the domain of the signature certificate is `engine.beacon.nist.gov`.

  - 1043 – $\langle optContext/{:}\mathrm{str}\rangle$ is a possibly empty string denoting an optional context. If not
    1044 empty it **CAN** be anything that is legal to appear in the *hier-part* (hierarchical
    1045 partitioning component) of a URL, but restricted to terminating with a front
    1046 slash character "/" and not containing the substring "chain/" nor the characters
    1047 "?" (used for queries) and "#" (used for fragments) — see Section 6 for details.

- 1048 • $\langle version{:}\mathrm{str}\rangle$ is the version number (as a UTF8 string), e.g., "2.0" or "2.0-beta1".

- 1049 • $\langle cid{:}\mathrm{dec}\rangle$ is the decimal representation of the integer value that appears in the `chainId`
  1050 field of the pulse.

- 1051 • $\langle pid{:}\mathrm{dec}\rangle$ is the decimal representation of the `pulseId` field of the pulse.

1052 **Recommendation:** when generating experimental (a.k.a. *beta*) pulses with the real signa-
1053 ture key, the $\langle optContext/\rangle$ sub-field **SHOULD** indicate the *beta* quality, possibly redundantly
1054 with the "beta" that appears in the `version` value.

1055 **4.2.2 Version**

1056 **Field name:** `version`

1057 **Default type:** verStr (a type of byte-string)

1058 **Relations:** its value must remain constant within each chain.

1059 **Description.** It is a variable-length string that indicates how to interpret the fields of the
1060 pulse. The value presented in this field is of the form 2.y, which is "2.0" in the version
1061 considered at the time of this writing.

1062 **Version updates requiring change of value.** Incrementing the value y **SHALL** happen
1063 when the pulse format is updated in a way that requires a pulse handling incompatible with
1064 the previous version, e.g., if adding or changing the order of fields used as input to the
1065 hash() used in the calculation of the pulse signature signatureValue or the output value
1066 randOut.

1067 **Identifying beta versions.** The ⟨version⟩ value **SHOULD** contain the string "beta" when-
1068 ever producing experimental pulses with a signature that uses the same key as used to to
1069 be used with non-beta pulses. For example, "2.0-beta" or "2.0-beta1" and/or "2.0-beta2"
1070 would denote version values used for beta testing. This allows repetition of values of
1071 chain—pulse indices while doing tests (which **MAY** involve creating real signatures). The
1072 "beta" expression signals users that such pulses **MAY** contain errors due to experimental
1073 procedures, including not obeying promises relating to timing or index-uniqueness.

1074 **Sub-versioning updates.** As previously mentioned, some minor updates of the beacon
1075 reference **MAY** refer to a sub-version that is not reflected in the version or uri fields. These
1076 updates, which refer to component z within 2.y.z, do not interfere with the interpretation of
1077 any previous pulses. This includes adding a specification for interpreting a new (previously
1078 undefined) value of the statusCode or cipherSuite fields. Those sub-version upgrades
1079 **MAY** require updating software for better parsing of new values, but must not imply any loss
1080 or invalidation of the relations between previous pulses within the same version value 2.y.

1081 Consider that some version 2.0.z defines how to interpret the first n bit-flags of field
1082 statusCode, and that the $n + 1^{th}$ through the m bit-flags are open for definition in future
1083 versions. Then, a software built for version 2.0.z **CAN** simply ignore those flags, or output
1084 a warning if/when detecting that they are filled with non-default values in a pulse with
1085 version=2.0.

1086 Consider that a new cipher value is defined in a sub-version update. Since cipher
1087 **CANNOT** change within a chain, the update does not interfere with the parsing of any pulses
1088 continuing from a pre-existing chain. If a software for version 2.0.w encounters an unknown
1089 cipher value, then it **SHOULD** output a corresponding informative warning/error to the user.

1090 **Remark (version in the NIST beacon).** In the initial NIST Beacon implementation
1091 of version 2.0, the pulses of chain 1 used value "Version 2.0" in the version field. The

23

1092   prefix "Version " is to be discontinued; the second chain of the NIST Beacon corrected
1093   the version value to simply "2.0".

1094   4.2.3   Cipher Suite

1095   **Field name:**   cipherSuite or (abbreviated) cipher

1096   **Default type:**   uint32

1097   **Relations:**   its value must remain constant within each chain.

1098   **Description.**   It is a 32-bit integer used to indicate which cryptographic standards are used
1099   for the hash function and signature. Table 4 describes the existing attributions for defined
1100   cipherSuite values. At present, only value 0 is defined.

Table 4. Attributions defined for cipherSuite

cipherSuite value	Hash function		Signature standard	
	Name	Byte length ($BLenHash$)	Name	Byte length ($BLenSig$)
0	SHA512 [NIS15]	64	RSA with PKCS 1.5 padding [NIS13a] (but allowing more keys sizes	$256+i$, for some $i \in \mathbb{N}_0$

The outputs of both hash function and signature algorithms are represented as big-endian integers and are serialized as byte strings. The hash function is defined for all uses of hash(), including in the signature. For each signature key, the signature length $BLenSig$ is fixed as the length of the RSA modulus. Note that using only 2048 bits (=256 bytes) for RSA is not considered enough to provide 128 bits of security.

1101   The hash function is represented as hash(), such that hash(x) is the hash of some
1102   byte-string serialized input x. The signature function is represented as SIGN(,), such that
1103   SIGN(SK,H) uses the signing key SK to produce the signature of a message whose hash
1104   (using hash()) is H.

1105   4.2.4   Period

1106   **Field name:**   period

1107   **Default type:**   uint32

1108   **Description.**   Is is a 32-bit unsigned integer that specifies the number of milliseconds of
1109   increment between the timeStamp values of two consecutive pulses when there are no gaps.
1110   The pulsating period of a chain is sometimes represented with symbol π.

1111 **Relations:** its value must remain constant within each chain; for example, if the *period* of
1112 a chain is one minute, then all pulses of that chain will have $\pi = 60,000$ (sixty thousand).

1113 4.3 Indexation fields

1114 The indexation fields allow identifying a pulse with respect to its order and position with the
1115 sequence(s) of generated pulses.

1116 4.3.1 Chain Index

1117 **Field name:** `chainIndex` or (abbreviated) `chainId`

1118 **Default type:** uint64

1119 **Description.** It is the positive integer index of the *chain* to which this pulse belongs. It has
1120 value 1 for the initial chain of each Beacon administrative domain implementing the Beacon
1121 reference version 2. The chain index is incremented by 1 for each new chain.

1122 **Relations.** The values in the fields `version`, `cipherSuite` and `period` **SHALL** be invari-
1123 ant within each chain. This implies in particular that any new value in any of these fields
1124 must happen in the first pulse of a new chain.

1125   Also, a chain **SHALL NOT** continue if the Beacon, e.g., due to some malfunctioning,
1126 loses the ability to ensure certain needed relation across the sequence of pulses. For example,
1127 a Beacon **SHALL NOT** continue a chain if it **CANNOT** produce a new pulse that satisfies the
1128 defined hash-chaining properties related to past output values within the chain.

1129 4.3.2 Pulse Index

1130 **Field name:** `pulseIndex` or (abbreviated) `pulseId`

1131 **Default type:** uint64

1132 **Description.** It is the positive integer index of this pulse within its chain. The first pulse of
1133 each chain has index 1, and each new pulse in each chain increments `pulseId` by 1.

1134 4.3.3 Timestamp

1135 **Field name:** `timeStamp` or (abbreviated) `time`

1136 **Default type:** dateStr (a type of byte string)

1137 **Description.** It contains a timestamp, representing a time instant, in the Universal Time
1138 Coordinated (UTC) standard, rather than in local time.

1139   As mentioned in Section 3.3, the timeStamp in a pulse does not represent the exact
1140 release time, but rather the promised time before which the Beacon engine does not release
1141 the pulse (see Promise 1), and the reference for other time limits on release (see Promise 4)
1142 and generation start (see Promise 3).

1143 **Format.** The value in the timeStamp field is represented as a string with 24 single-byte
1144 characters, following the format in RFC3339 [NK02]:

$$\langle year \rangle - \langle month \rangle - \langle day \rangle \texttt{T} \langle hour \rangle : \langle minute \rangle : \langle second \rangle . \langle millisecond \rangle \texttt{Z} \qquad (11)$$

1145   The string is composed by a *date*, followed by an identifier character "T" (denoting that
1146 a time of day will follow), then by the *time of day*, and finally by a character "Z" (denoting
1147 "Zulu", meaning the zero hours zone, which identifies the UTC format).

1148   The date is a 10-byte string, composed of three numeric components — a 4-digit *year*, a
1149 2-digit *month* and a 2-digit *day* — separated by a dash "-". The time of day is a 13-byte
1150 string composed of four numeric components — a 2-digit *hour*, a 2-digit *minute*, a 2-digit
1151 *second* and a 3-digit *millisecond* components — the first three separated by a colon ":" and
1152 the last one separated by a dot ".". For example:

1153   • the timestamp 1945-06-26T16:59:11.000Z identifies the date of signing the United Na-
1154   tions Charter, on June 06, 1945, at the UTC time 16 hours, 59 minutes and 11 seconds.

1155   • the timestamp 2019-01-01T00:00:00.000Z identifies the starting instant of the year
1156   2019, in UTC time, up to millisecond precision.

1157 The beacon format requires pulses to always use this format in the timeStamp field, includ-
1158 ing the "T" and "Z" characters, and the seconds and milliseconds components.

1159   When serializing fields, an integer is also used to describe the number of bytes (24) of
1160 characters used to express the timeStamp string.

1161 **Abbreviation.** For improved readability, in the remainder of this document we often use
1162 an abbreviated format for timestamps. This is specially useful since we adopt as default
1163 examples cases where timestamps have the second and millisecond components equal to
1164 0. In such cases, we use a space (" ") instead of "T", and omits the seconds, milliseconds,
1165 and "Z". For example, for a beacon that pulsates with a period of 1 minute, and whose
1166 *promises* establish the minute mark as the allowed release time for pulses, we CAN say in
1167 this document, but not in the actual pulses, that the timestamps

2020-01-01 00:00
2020-01-01 01:01
2020-01-01 02:02

1168 are expected to be the first ones to appear in the year 2020. However, the actual timestamps
1169 in the corresponding pulses SHALL be written as

$$2020\text{-}01\text{-}01\text{T}00\text{:}00\text{:}00.000\text{Z}$$
$$2020\text{-}01\text{-}01\text{T}01\text{:}01\text{:}00.000\text{Z}$$
$$2020\text{-}01\text{-}01\text{T}02\text{:}02\text{:}00.000\text{Z}.$$

1170 **Relations.** If T is the timestamp in a pulse, then $T - \pi$ and $T + \pi$ are the previous and the
1171 next timestamps, if there are no time-gaps.

4.3.4 Status

1173 **Field name:** `statusCode` or (abbreviated) `status`

1174 **Default type:** uint32

1175 **Description.** It is a sequence of 32 bits (a.k.a. *bit flags*), indicating the current status of the
1176 chain. Each flag indicates some aspect of the status, as defined in Table 5. The ordering (1st,
1177 2nd,..., 32th) of flags is from right to left, to match the ordering of least significant bits (LSBs)
1178 of the 32-bit unsigned integer corresponding to the (big-endian) serialization of the bit-vector.

1179 **Detailed explanation.** In the current Beacon reference version (2.0.0), only the four
1180 right-most flags are defined with a fixed meaning. All other flags are by default set to
1181 0, unless if/when possibly defining a new meaning for them. The 5th through the 16th
1182 rightmost flags are reserved for future sub-versions (including 2.0.z) or versions (2.y.z) of
1183 the beacon format. The 17th through the 32nd rightmost flags are reserved for individual
1184 beacon operators to define. The definition of the latter require that a description be available
1185 for users — see corresponding interface call (5k) in Section 6.6

1186 **Example values.** Let `0bX...X` be a sequence of bits X...X, where the ith X, counting
1187 from right to left, represents the ith LSB of (i.e., with additive weight 2^{i-1} in the) integer
1188 value `status`. Compared with an enumeration of all possible `status` integer values, the
1189 specification using bit-flags is specially useful considering that the number of possible
1190 combinations grow exponentially with the number of flags. We enumerate several special
1191 examples:

- `status = 0b0 = 0`: Indicates a normal transition since the previous pulse in the chain:
  without a time gap; without a change of `certId`; with `randLocal` being well related
  to the `preCom` in the previous pulse; with more pulses being expected for this chain.

- `status = 0b1 = 1`: The `randLocal` value does not correspond to a previous `preCom`
  in the chain. In an ideal functioning, this status occurs only if this pulse is the first

Table 5. Bit-flags of the `status` field

LSB	Variable name	What?	if set (1)	if unset (0)	Possible values in the 1st pulse of a chain
1st	FLS_rndloc	`randLocal` without corresponding `preCom` in chain?	yes	no	1
2nd	FLS_gap	Gap in chain?	yes	no	0
3rd	FLS_certid	`certId` changed in chain?	yes	no	0
4th	FLS_end	End of chain?	yes	no	0
5th–16th	—	Reserved for definition in future versions	—	—	—
17th–32th	—	Reserved for local definition (per beacon)	—	—	—

LSB = least significant bit. The FLS prefix indicates a flag of the `status` field.

in a chain. However, an abnormal functioning of a Beacon CAN lead to a non-first pulse with this status code, if the sequence of pulses would not have gaps and at the same time the field `randOut` was not populated (i.e., was filled with all zeros). Such abnormal case SHOULD warrant an external application to invalidate the pulse for the purpose of combining beacons (see Section 7.4).

- status = 0b10 = 2: The pulse follows after a gap without loss of randLocal — whenever the previous pulse has a `timeStamp` value more than one period (π) away in the past, and `randLocal` is still related as expected with the `preCom` of the previous pulse in the chain.

- status = 0b11 = 3: The pulse follows after gap with loss of randLocal — whenever the previous pulse has a `timeStamp` value more than one period (π) away in the past and the hash pre-images of the previous `preCom` as been lost. In this case the field `randLocal` is filled with an all-zeros string.

- status = 0b100 = 4: The value `certId` in a non-staring pulse (i.e., with `pulseId` > 1) has changed since the previous pulse in the chain.

- status = 0b1000 = 8: The pulse is, by purposed planning, the last in the chain.

- status = 0b1010 = 10: The pulse follows after a gap and is marked as the last in the chain.

Notes.

- There is no flag identifying the beginning of a chain; that property CAN already be determined from checking `pulseId` $\stackrel{?}{=} 1$.

28

1218　　　• Even though FL_rndloc is equal to 1 in the first pulse of a chain, the field randLocal
1219　　　　in a new chain MAY still be filled with the pre-image of preCom of the (last) pulse
1220　　　　of another chain.

1221　　　• The requirement that the first pulse of a chain has FL_end = 0 intends to enforce that
1222　　　　chains are composed of more than one pulse.

1223 **Flags for local definitions.**   The definition of local flags must preserve the syntax of all
1224 remaining aspects of pulses. For example, a Beacon MAY specify (one or more) flags to:

1225　　　• represent some information about the use of RNGs, e.g., whether or not more than
1226　　　　two RNGs have been sampled;

1227　　　• indicate information about the generation-start timing, e.g., using 8 bits to encode the
1228　　　　number of seconds in advance at which the local randomness was sampled;

1229　　　• indicate whether the certificate in use has expired;

1230　　　• indicate whether the signing key has changed in comparison with the previous pulse.

1231 **Use-case.**   The status field is specially useful to indicate when there is something
1232 irregular or unusual about the chain between the previous and current pulse. For certain
1233 applications, the statusCode field may be useful to signal to users whether the pulse is
1234 acceptable for use or not. For example, when combining pulses from different beacons,
1235 it may be necessary to require that there were no previous gaps and that the randLocal
1236 is correct. This CAN be easily filtered by checking that the 1st and 2nd LSBs are 0, without
1237 prejudice of then performing other necessary verifications.

1238 **4.4 The local random value**

1239 **Field name:** localRandomValue cr (abbreviated) randLocal

1240 **Default type:** hashOut

1241 **Relations.** It is the hash() preimage of the preCom value output in the previous pulse. In
1242 the first pulse of a chain it is filled with an all-zeros string.

1243 **Description.** It is a 512-bit value with 512 bits* of entropy, generated by the Beacon
1244 engine during the process of generation of the previous pulse, but kept secret from the
1245 outside until its release. (* Actually, since the value is the output of a cryptographic-hash
1246 function, the actual entropy MAY forfeit up to less than one bit of entropy, while remaining
1247 indistinguishable from uniformly random.)

1248　　　The randLocal must be entirely unpredictable to any attacker outside the beacon
1249 engine. By convention, it is the result of hashing with hash() the concatenation of two or

1250   more 512-bit random values from independent sources. For example, if the beacon has
1251   three independent random bit generators providing random numbers ρ_1, ρ_2, ρ_3, then

$$\texttt{randLocal} = \texttt{hash}(\rho_1 \parallel \rho_2 \parallel \rho_3). \tag{12}$$

1252   The combination of randomness from several RNGs brings an important security ad-
1253   vantage. Even if all but one RNGs fail or are malicious, the resulting `randLocal` is still a
1254   high-quality random number. For example, any RNG providing good randomness prevents
1255   any malicious RNG from exfiltrating information via the `randLocal` field. However, there
1256   is no way for a user of the Beacon to determine whether `randLocal` has been calculated
1257   from a correct combination of randomness sampled from several RNGs.

1258   **Remark (On the timing of learning `randLocal`).** For the purpose of the timing of pulse
1259   generation, the beginning of generation of each pulse corresponds to the starting moment
1260   of sampling of the RNGs. In the current design, the `randLocal` value is then obtained by
1261   the Beacon App, still before the actual pulse output (`randOut`) is calculated. Section 8.3.1
1262   mentions a conceivable alternative (for future versions), where the `randLocal` value would
1263   be calculated in a different way, satisfying a different relation with `preCom`, such that it
1264   could only be obtained after the end of the pulse generation, and such that it could not be
1265   fully decided even by a malicious Beacon operator.

1266   **Guidance (gaps with loss of local random value).** Very rarely, the Beacon engine **MAY**
1267   suffer a memory failure such that the pre-generated `randLocal` value is lost. In this case, if
1268   the chain continues then the next pulse will fill `randLocal` with all-zeros and the 2nd bit
1269   flag of the `status` field will be set to 1 (see Table 5).

1270   It is not expected that pre-generated `randLocal` value is lost without the occurrence
1271   of a gap. Such conceivable event would represent, for a non-starting pulse, an abnormal
1272   condition marked with a status value 1.

4.5 External value fields

1274   The format 2.0 for pulses specifies three fields — `ext.srcId`, `ext.status`, `ext.value` —
1275   that support the inclusion of a verifiable external source of entropy. Using an external source
1276   enables providing strong assurance, to the outside world, that even a malicious beacon
1277   could have not computed far ahead in the past the output values (`randOut`) of pulses.

1278   **Informal summary.** The field `ext.value` **MAY** sometimes, optionally, be filled with the
1279   hash of a value generated by an external source. The hashing **CAN** be computed locally (e.g.,
1280   the hash of the results of public lotteries) or externally (e.g., if directly using the `randOut`
1281   value of another beacon, which is already a hash). The value **SHOULD** be obtained according

1282 to a description whose hash() is recorded in the field ext.srcId. Certain aspects of the use
1283 of the external source are indicated by corresponding elements of the ext.status field.

1284   The purpose of the ext.value field is to introduce some value that is outside the control
1285 of the beacon operator, is hard to predict before a certain moment in time, and is relatively
1286 easy for anyone to verify after the fact. For example, a given beacon might use the hash of the
1287 closing prices of some stock market, the hash of the winning lottery numbers from diverse
1288 state lotteries, or the hash of every thousandth block of some popular public blockchain.
1289 For proper usability and security, there must be no ambiguity, given the text hashed by
1290 ext.srcId, about the correct value of ext.value.

1291   While the use of external sources is optional, the three fields are always present. When,
1292 upon starting a new chain, an external value has not been previously used, the fields
1293 ext.value and ext.srcId are filed with all zeros, i.e., with ZeroH. Once an external value
1294 is used for the first time, the same value CAN be repeated in subsequent pulses until a new
1295 external value is used. The repetition is useful since it continues giving to those standalone
1296 pulses an element that enables proving that the pulse generation did not happen before the
1297 existence of the external value, i.e., without need to show relations to a previous pulse.

1298   It can be useful to identify whether the external value in a pulse appeared for the first
1299 time in that pulse or in a previous one. It is in the first use that such value is most relevant
1300 with respect to mitigating a pre-computation attack by a malicious beacon. For that reason
1301 the ext.status field contains one flag used to indicate when the ext.value has changed.
1302 As a complementary relational feature, the pulse MAY also show, optionally, in part of its
1303 ext.status field, the pulseId of the first pulse which used the same value of ext.value.

4.5.1 External source identifier

1305 **Field name:** external.sourceId or (abbreviated) ext.srcId

1306 **Field type:** hashOut

1307 **Relations:** ext.value = hash(ext.TextSrcDesc)

1308   (Notice that ext.TextSrcDesc is not a pulse field.)

1309 **Description.** It is filled with the hash() of a MIME type text/plain document, encoded as
1310 a UTF8 string (ext.TextSrcDesc), describing the external source of entropy, including
1311 instructions for updating ext.value. When an external source is not used in a pulse, the
1312 field is set to ZeroH.

1313   To allow complete verification of all pulses, the text description of any source identifier
1314 ever used by the Beacon SHALL be available to users. Section 6.5 defines an interface
1315 call (4m) that specifies how users CAN obtain the text description ext.TextSrcDesc
1316 corresponding to a ext.srcId value.

1317　**Requirement.**

1318　　　• **Encoding of text description.** The description text (ext.TextSrcId) **SHALL** be spec-
1319　　　　ified as a UTF8 string. Is is used directly as the input of hash(), used to compute
1320　　　　`ext.srcId`, being interpreted directly as a byte-string (each UTF8 character **MAY**
1321　　　　be between 1 and 4 bytes long). Notice that here we do not apply `Byt_serialize_-`
1322　　　　`string`, which would otherwise prefix the byte length of the text description.

1323　**Recommendations.** A definition of an external source **SHOULD** specify several attributes:

1324　　　1. **External source (text description):** a short description of the type of value.

1325　　　2. **Intended update frequency:** the expected frequency with which the `ext.value`
1326　　　　field will be updated with respect to this source.

1327　　　3. **Intended update moment:** the first timestamp intended for each new `ext.value`.

1328　　　4. **Repeat until new available value (yes/no):** a "yes" or "no" answer to whether
1329　　　　the value `ext.value` **SHOULD** continue repeating, in opposition to reverting to an
1330　　　　all-zeros string, until a new external value is available for update.

1331　　　5. **Local hashing (yes/no):** whether the Beacon needs to hash the value obtained from
1332　　　　the external source. By default, we assume that external values **SHOULD** be hashed.
1333　　　　However, this **CAN** be avoided if the value is already described as a suitable hash out-
1334　　　　put of an externally obtainable pre-image. For example, this is the case if the external
1335　　　　source value is the `randOut` value of some other compliant beacon. In that case, not
1336　　　　doing local hashing has the benefits of allowing an easier external search for any used
1337　　　　`ext.value`, and allowing an easier verification by the user (e.g., side-by-side com-
1338　　　　parison of the `randOut` in one beacon vs. the `external.value` in another beacon).

1339　　　6. **Default URL for access (uriStr):** the expected URL from which users **CAN** obtain
1340　　　　information about the value and authenticity of the pre-image of the used `ext.value`.

1341　　　7. **Recommended sampling trials (string):** when to retry sampling, if initial trials fail.

1342　　　8. **Fall back options:** what to do if the external source is unavailable beyond a
1343　　　　reasonable time window.

1344　**A sketch example of a source identifier — Output values from an external beacon.**
1345　"External source: from the Chilean Beacon (https://beacon.clcert.cl/), the output value
1346　(`randOut`) of the pulse with largest `timeStamp` value with ⟨hour⟩ component not larger than
1347　12. Intended update frequency: daily. Intended update moment: for every "15:00:00.000"
1348　UTC time mark, update the external value in the first (local) pulse with `timeStamp` with
1349　⟨hour⟩ component not smaller than 15. Repeat until new available value: yes. Local hashing:
1350　no. Default URL for access: https://beacon.clcert.cl/beacon/2.0/time/previous/⟨date⟩-
1351　12:00:00.001Z" where ⟨date⟩ is the current day if sampled after 15:00:00.000. Recom-

1352 mended sampling trials: starting at 12:05, sample the external source once every 5 minutes
1353 until obtaining randOut of a pulse with timeStamp not inferior to 12:00. Fall back options:
1354 None. (Always use the latest randOut value of the external beacon obtained from the
1355 recommended trials.)

1356   The definition of an external source SHOULD be precise and careful. We currently defer
1357 those definitions to a future addendum or separate document, and simply enumerate here, in
1358 high-level, a few other examples of conceivable sources:

1359 • *stock markets* — the closing index of some stock market, from the current trading
1360   day, e.g., updated at 23:00 local time on trading days (not on holidays).

1361 • *time synchronization information* — the recorded offsets between national official
1362   clocks across many countries, with respect to a universally accepted global clock,
1363   possibly updated once an hour.

1364 • *independently run lotteries* — results from national lotteries occurring at predictable
1365   days, across several states or countries.

1366 • *seismic or weather data sources* — using structured data from a reliable publisher
1367   that allows search of corresponding historical data.

1368 **Additional aspects.** A more detailed set of recommendations and examples is deferred to
1369 a future separate document.

1370 ### 4.5.2   External Status

1371 **Field name:**   external.statusCode or (abbreviated) ext.status

1372 **Default type.** uint64

1373 **Description.** It is a sequence of 64 bits, informing aspects of the status of the use of
1374 an external source. It provides useful information on how to interpret the use of fields
1375 ext.srcId and ext.value.

1376 **Serialization.** When part of a hash input, it is serialized as a 64-bit unsigned integer.
1377 However, for ease of reference it CAN be described as a pair of 32-bit unsigned integers: the
1378 first, of optional filling, represents the index of the first pulse that used the same ext.value
1379 — if not filled it is set to ZeroH. the second represents a sequence of 32 bit-flags denoting
1380 aspects of the status of the use of an external source. In the latter, the ordering (1st, 2nd,...,
1381 32th) of flags is from right to left, to match the ordering of least significant bits (LSBs) of
1382 the 64-bit unsigned integer corresponding to the (big-endian) serialization of the bit-vector.

1383 **Example values.** Let 0bX...X be a sequence of bits X...X, where the ith X, counting from
1384 right to left, represents the ith LSB of (i.e., with additive weight 2^{i-1} in) the integer value

Table 6. Bit-flags of the `ext.status` field

LSB	Variable name	What?	if set (1)	if unset (0)
1st	FLE_extValUsed	External value is used in this pulse?	yes	no
2th	FLE_SrcIdChan	ext.srcId has changed?	yes	no
3th	FLE_extValChan	ext.value has changed?	yes	no
4th	FL_extValOld	ext.value failed to update?	yes	no
5th	FLE_WhyOld	A missed update is internal fault?	yes	no
6rd	FLE_RegNewSrcId	Registration of new ext.srcId?	yes	no
7th–15th	—	Reserved for future definition	—	—
16th	FLE_showsFirstPid	Is ext.FistPidSameExt filled?	yes	no
17th–32th	—	Reserved for local definition (per Beacon)	—	—
33th–64th	ext.FistPidSameExt	pulseId (a 32-bit index) of the first pulse with same ext.value	(Optional use)	

LSB = least significant bit. The FLE prefix indicates a flag of the `ext.status` field.

1385　`ext.status`. We enumerate several examples:

1386　• `ext.status` = 0b0 = 0: No external value used; implies that `ext.value` and
1387　　`ext.srcId` are all zeros.

1388　• `ext.status` = 0b1 = 1: `ext.value` is in use (1st flag is 1), filled with a (possibly
1389　　hashed) value obtained from an external source, either in repetition (4th flag is 0) or
1390　　being in the first pulse in the chain (4rd flag is 0).

1391　• `ext.status` = 0b10 = 2: The `ext.srcId` field is filled with a new value, but there
1392　　is no corresponding value in the `ext.value` field. This case is used to signal to users
1393　　that the new `ext.srcId` value is the identifier of a new potential source, to be used
1394　　later. This is called a registration of a new `ext.srcId`.

1395　• `ext.status` = 0b1001 = 9: The `ext.value` in use (FLE_extValUsed = 1) was
1396　　supposed to have already changed (FL_extValOld = 1), but it has not changed due
1397　　to some external problem (FLE_WhyOld = 0).

1398　• `ext.status` = 0x11 0000 8001 = $17 \cdot 2^{32} + 2^{15} + 2^0$: The current `ext.value`
1399　　appeared in this chain for the first time in the pulse with `pulseId` = 0x11 = 17.

1400　**Recommendation (registration of new external source identifier).** It is convenient to
1401　limit `ext.srcId` to be filled with values previously announced to users. For that purpose,
1402　whenever a new source identifier *scrNew* is devised by a Beacon, it **SHOULD** first be
1403　registered in a pulse, by issuing a pulse with `ext.srcId` = *scrNew*, `ext.value` = ZeroH

1404 and FLE_RegNewSrcId = 1. From that point onward, it becomes "non-surprising" to have an
1405 external value filled in ext.value, with a corresponding source Id ext.srcId = *scrNew*.

1406 **Flags for local definitions.**   The current definition of the external.statusCode field
1407 allows 16 bits to be defined locally by each beacon. This CAN for example be used to
1408 indicate additional useful information about how to interpret information of external values,
1409 or external source descriptions. For example, a beacon MAY decide to use several bits to
1410 indicate with more detail the reason for a missed update of an external value.

1411 4.5.3 External Value

1412 **Field name:**   external.value or (abbreviated) ext.value

1413 **Default type.** hashOut

1414 **Description.** It is filled with the hash() of the sampled value of an external source of entropy
1415 whose description is committed (by a hash) in the ext.srcId field. The sampled value
1416 must be encoded as a UTF8 string, and used directly as the input of hash(), when used to
1417 compute ext.value, being interpreted directly as a byte-string (each UTF8 character MAY
1418 be between 1 and 4 bytes long). Notice that here we do not apply Byt_serialize_string,
1419 which would otherwise prefix the byte length of the text description.

1420   Since the use of an external source is optional, when not in use the fields ext.value,
1421 ext.status and ext.srcId are set to zero (e.g., a string of integers zero when serialized
1422 as a byte-string).

1423 4.6   Fields with past output values

1424 The previous beacon format (1.0) had a single field (previous) containing the outputValue
1425 value of a past pulse (the previous one). This ensured that the sequence of pulses formed a
1426 hash chain. The new beacon format has five such fields, in order to support more efficient
1427 ways of proving consistency between pulses. These values are maintained within a single
1428 chain of pulses (that is, the sequence of pulses with the same chainId value from a given
1429 beacon operator).

1430   The extra named fields permit a very efficient proof of an intact hash chain between
1431 pulses at any two timestamps T_1 and T_2, as will be further discussed in Section 5.

1432 4.6.1   Previous

1433 **Field name:**   previous or out.Prev.

1434 **Field type.** hashOut

1435　**Description.** It is filled with the randOut value of the previous pulse. This field ensures
1436　that an unbroken sequence of pulses forms a hash chain. If the most recent pulse in the
1437　chain is known, an alteration of any earlier pulse in the chain CAN be easily detected. This
1438　hash-chaining ensure that even the beacon operator has no power to rewrite the history
1439　previous to a known pulse.

1440　**Chain-start values.** When a new chain starts, if possible the previous field SHOULD be
1441　filled with the value in the randOut field of the last pulse of the previous chain. All other
1442　past-output fields (out.H, out.D, out.M, out.Y) are set to ZeroH.

1443　### 4.6.2　Hour, Day, Month and Year

1444　Each pulse replicates, besides the previous output value (out.Prev), several other past
1445　output values chosen in accordance to a relation of time values. Concretely, each pulse with
1446　index (pulseId) i includes the first representative pulse of each UTC timestamp component
1447　related to the timestamp of the previous pulse (i.e., with pulseId $= i - 1$). There are four
1448　such fields, corresponding to the time components *hour*, *day*, *month* and *year*.

1449　**Field names:** hour or out.H; day or out.D; month or out.M; year or out.Y.

1450　**Field types.** hashOut

1451　**Description:** Each pulse replicates several past output values, i.e., the randOut value from
1452　past previous pulses. For each of the named fields $x \in \{\text{hour}, \text{month}, \text{day}, \text{year}\}$, the past
1453　pulse from which to collect the randOut value is chosen as follows:

1454　　　1. Look at the UTC timestamp T' of the pulse *previous* to the current one.

1455　　　2. Let T'' be the first timestamp, present in some past pulse, whose truncation down to the
1456　　　　precision of the x component (*hour*, *month*, *day* or *year*) is equal to the corresponding
1457　　　　truncation of T'.

1458　　　3. Fill $P[T].x$ with value $P[T''].$randOut. More concretely:

1459　　　　　• year gets randOut from the first pulse with timeStamp with the same UTC
1460　　　　　　*year* as the timeStamp of the previous pulse.

1461　　　　　• month gets randOut from the first pulse with timeStamp with the same UTC
1462　　　　　　*year* and ***month*** and as the timeStamp of the previous pulse.

1463　　　　　• day gets randOut from the first pulse with timeStamp with the same UTC *year*,
1464　　　　　　*month* and ***day*** as the timeStamp of the previous pulse.

1465　　　　　• hour gets randOut from the first pulse with timeStamp with the same UTC
1466　　　　　　*year*, *month*, *day* and ***hour*** as the timeStamp of the previous pulse.

1467   In other words, for any field $\langle x \rangle \in \{$hour, day, month, year$\}$, the value $\langle x \rangle_i$ (i.e., $P_i.\langle x \rangle$)
1468 is filled with the randOut$_j$, where j is the pulseId of the first pulse whose truncation
1469 of timeStamp, down to the precision of the time component $\langle x \rangle$, equals the correspond-
1470 ing truncation of timeStamp$_{i-1}$. For example, year$_i$ = outputValue$_j$, where j is the
1471 pulseIndex value in the first pulse whose UTC **year** in timeStamp$_j$ is equal to the UTC
1472 **year** of timeStamp$_{i-1}$.

1473 **Values in beginning of a chain.** In the first pulse of a chain:

1474   • The values out.H, out.D, out.M, and out.Y start out as ZeroH.

1475   • When possible, the field out.Prev **SHOULD** be filled with the randOut of the previ-
1476   ous chain, if it is available; otherwise, previous **MAY** also start as zeros.

1477   In the second pulse of a chain, every one of the past output value fields (out.Prev,
1478 out.H, out.D, out.M, out.Y) is filled with the value of the randOut field in the first pulse,
1479 since that pulse is the *first* pulse of the chain with the same hour, day, month, and year as the
1480 previous (i.e., the first) pulse.

1481 **Conceivable future update of format.** Various Beacons or chains **MAY** have different
1482 pulsating period. If as part of a chain a Beacon outputs a pulse once every 5 seconds, then
1483 the corresponding skiplists could be more efficient if the hash chaining also included the
1484 output value of the first pulse with the minute equal to the previous pulse. Correspondingly,
1485 if a Beacon outputs once every day, then the fields previous, hour and day would become
1486 redundant and the chain would be more efficient by removing the hour and day fields.
1487 Considering the above, it is conceivable a future update that enables some flexibility on
1488 the choice, for each chain, of which past pulses are selected, and including indexations
1489 fields (e.g., pulseId and time) for the included past pulses.

1490 ### 4.6.3 Example without gaps

1491 The box on the right shows an example
1492 of how to fill the fields of past output val-
1493 ues, when there is no interference from
1494 time gaps. We consider as example a chain
1495 whose first pulse was issued with timestamp
1496 2018-07-23 19:26.

> **Example for** $P[$2018-11-22 16:32$]$
>
> previous $\leftarrow P[$2018-11-22 16:31$]$.randOut
> hour $\leftarrow P[$2018-11-22 16:00$]$.randOut
> day $\leftarrow P[$2018-11-22 00:00$]$.randOut
> month $\leftarrow P[$2018-11-01 00:00$]$.randOut
> year $\leftarrow P[$2018-07-23 19:26$]$.randOut

1497   The only unexpected value is for the out.Y field, which does not have a date of 2018-
1498 01-01 (January 01, 2018) because the first pulse of the chain as a posterior date.

1499   4.6.4   Example with skipped pulses

1500 Beacons SHOULD be operational most of the time, but hardware failures, software failures,
1501 power outages, and other problems CAN occur from time to time, and so there are times
1502 when pulses MAY be skipped. This introduces some complexity in the rule for determining
1503 the value in fields hour, day, month, and year.

1504   The general rule is to start from the timeStamp of the *previous* pulse, and then determine
1505 the first pulse in that hour, day, month, and year. However, the first pulse in an hour MAY
1506 have a timestamp with a minute component different from **00**.

1507 **Example with consecutive skipped pulses.** Consider
1508 the example on the right, with a time-gap between
1509 2018-12-26 16:08 and 2019-01-22 13:24. This time-gap ex-
1510 isted in the chain with index 1 of the NIST Randomness Bea-
1511 con version 2, due to a U.S. Government shutdown. The men-
1512 tioned gap means that after the issued pulse with timestamp
1513 2018-12-26 16:07 (and pulseId = 220, 394) several expected
1514 pulses were skipped, such that the subsequent issued pulse has
1515 timestamp 2019-01-22 13:25 (and pulseId = 220, 395).

2018-07-23 **19:26**
2018-07-23 **19:27**
⋮
2018-12-26 **16:06**
2018-12-26 **16:07**
[Gap (skipped pulses)]
2019-01-28 13:25
2019-01-28 13:**26**

1516   Assuming no other pulses have been skipped, we CAN determine the linking fields for
1517 the first two pulses after the outage. The existing relations are depicted in Fig. 5.

1518   • **First pulse after outage.** P[2019-01-28 **13:25**] is the first pulse produced after the
1519   exemplified outage. Highlighted in yellow background in Fig. 5 is the previous field,
1520   which was filled with the randOut value of the previous pulse, which had a surprising
1521   timestamp (because of the time gap). The link is to a pulse produced more than one
1522   month in the past, due to the exemplified outage. In relation to the previous pulse,
1523   all the other fields with past output values link to the output values of past pulses
1524   generated at the expected times. Specifically, they link to the first pulse produced in
1525   the {hour, day, month, year} specified in the timestamp of the *previous* pulse.

1526   • **Second pulse after outage.** P[2019-01-28 **13:26**] is the second pulse produced after
1527   the outage. In this case, the potentially surprising linking timestamps (highlighted in
1528   yellow in Fig. 5) are those used to populate the out.H, out.D, out.M and out.Y fields.
1529   Those four fields contain the same value, since the gap crossed the year boundary.

1530   4.6.5   If past output values are lost

1531 It is conceivable, although unexpected, that a memory problem in the Beacon App MAY
1532 lead it to lose access to the past output values needed for hash-chaining of each new pulse.
1533 The Beacon SHALL NOT continue the same chain without a proper hash-chaining of all
1534 those fields. Thus, it the Beacon operator wishes to continue the chain, it SHALL update the
1535 state of the Beacon App with information about the past pulses (which by then SHOULD be

Example: During a U.S. Government shutdown, the NIST Beacon had a gap in chain 1 between times 2018-12-26 16:08 and 2019-01-28 13:24.

1st pulse after gap: $P[\text{2019-}\textbf{01-28 13:25}]$	2nd pulse after gap: $P[\text{2019-}\textbf{01-28 13:26}]$
previous ← $P[\textbf{2018-12-26 16:07}]$.randOut	previous ← $P[\text{2019-01-28 13:25}]$.randOut
hour ← $P[\text{2018-12-26 16:}\textbf{00}]$.randOut	hour ← $P[\text{2019-01-28 13:}\textbf{25}]$.randOut
day ← $P[\text{2018-12-26 }\textbf{00:00}]$.randOut	day ← $P[\text{2019-01-28 13:}\textbf{25}]$.randOut
month ← $P[\text{2018-12-}\textbf{01 00:00}]$.randOut	month ← $P[\text{2019-01-28 13:}\textbf{25}]$.randOut
year ← $P[\text{2018-}\textbf{07-23 19:26}]$.randOut	year ← $P[\text{2019-01-28 13:}\textbf{25}]$.randOut

Figure 5. Obtaining past output values after gaps

1536 externally known, since they had already been released to the Beacon databases and possibly
1537 queried from the outside). This update is contrary to the usual logical flow of information,
1538 which is supposed to be unilateral between the Beacon Engine and the database of pulses.

1539 ## 4.7 The precommitment value

1540 **Field name:** precommitmentValue or (abbreviated) preCom

1541 **Default type:** hashOut

1542 **Relations:** The field is defined as $P_i.\texttt{preCom} = \texttt{hash}(P_{i+1}.\texttt{randLocal})$

1543 **Description:** It is a hash commitment to the *next* pulse's randLocal. This requires the
1544 beacon to know randLocal of the *next* pulse before *this* pulse is output. The purpose of the
1545 field is to facilitate combining of outputs from multiple beacons, as discussed in Section 7.4.

1546 **Guidance (simple gaps).** When there is a gap in the sequence of pulses, the beacon engine
1547 **SHOULD** have the next localRandomValue value stored. Under most circumstances, then,
1548 the next pulse, even if it appears after a lengthy gap in the sequence of pulses from the beacon,
1549 **SHOULD** have randLocal such that precommitmentValue = hash(localRandomValue).

1550 For example, suppose there is a sequence of pulses with
1551 timestamps as exemplified on the right, with a time-gap
1552 of with pulses skipped between 2019-01-22 01:13 and
1553 2019-01-22 05:24: Under normal circumstances, the beacon
1554 engine will have retained the randLocal value committed
1555 by $P[\text{2019-01-22 01:12}]$.preCom. In such case we will have:

2019-01-22 01:**11**
2019-01-22 01:**12**
[Gap (skipped pulses)]
2019-01-22 **05:25**
2019-01-22 05:**26**

$$P[\text{2019-01-22 }\textbf{01:12}].\texttt{preCom}] = \texttt{hash}(P[\text{2019-01-22 }\textbf{05:25}].\texttt{randLocal}) \qquad (13)$$

1556 and $P[\text{2019-01-22 05:25}]$.status $= 0b10$ will indicate that a time gap existed in the produc-
1557 tion of pulses and that the pre-image of precommitmentValue remained intact.

1558 **Guidance (gaps with loss of local random value).** Very rarely, the Beacon engine **MAY**
1559 suffer a catastrophic failure such that the pre-generated `randLocal` value is lost. In that case,
1560 $P[\text{2019-01-22 05:25}].$`status`$= \text{0b11}$ will indicate both a gap before 2019-01-22 05:25 and
1561 also a failure to reveal a pre-image of `preCom`. In this case, `randLocal` is set to all-zeros,
1562 implying $P[\text{2019-01-22 01:12}].$`preCom` $\neq$ `hash`$(P[\text{2019-01-22 05:25}].$`randLocal`$)$.

1563 ## 4.8 Signature-related fields

1564 ### 4.8.1 Signature

1565 **Field name:** `signatureValue` or (abbreviated) `sig`

1566 **Default type:** sigOut

1567 **Relations:** $F_{20,i} = \text{sig}_i = Sign_{SK}\left(\text{hash}\left(||_{k\in\{1,...,19\}}\overline{F_{k,i}}\right)\right)$; or, as a sequence of three steps:

$$Z \leftarrow \text{Byt\_serialize\_fields}(\langle\text{uri},\text{version},$$
$$\text{cipher},\text{period},\text{certId},\text{chainId},\text{pulseId},\text{time},$$
$$\text{randLocal},\text{ext.srcId},\text{ext.status},\text{ext.value},$$
$$\text{previous},\text{hour},\text{day},\text{month},\text{year},\text{preCom},\text{status}\rangle) \qquad (14)$$
$$H \leftarrow \text{hash}(Z) \qquad (15)$$
$$\text{sig} \leftarrow \text{SIGN}(SK,H), \text{ where } SK \text{ is the secret signing key.} \qquad (16)$$

1568 **Description:** A (cryptographic) digital signature of the `hash()` of a concatenation of the
1569 byte-serialization of all previous fields in the pulse. When `cipher` $= 0$, the value produced
1570 is an RSA signature using PKCSv1.5 padding, encoded unambiguously as a byte string (see
1571 Section 4.1.2).

1572   The signature allows a user to confirm that the pulse came from the beacon claimed in
1573 the `uri` field, and has not been altered since then. In the case of an attempt by the beacon
1574 operator to alter previous beacon pulses (aka, to rewrite history), the signature **CAN** be
1575 used to provide evidence of its misbehavior — the existence of a properly signed beacon
1576 pulse which is not on the chain of pulses is unambiguous evidence of misbehavior by the
1577 beacon. (It is not necessarily evidence of malfeasance, but it is unambiguous evidence that
1578 the beacon is not following the protocol.)

1579 ### 4.8.2 Certificate ID

1580 **Field name:** `certificateId` or (abbreviated) `certId`

1581 **Default type:** hashOut

1582 **Description.**   It is the `hash()` of a Base 64 encoded PEM formatted file (X.509 ASN.1
1583 encoding), following the RFC 5280 [CSF+08] specification, containing the certificate(s)
1584 of the public counter-part of the Beacon signing key used to produce the value in the
1585 `signatureValue` field of the pulse. The signing key must always have a corresponding
1586 certificate, even if it is self-signed. However, it is recommended that certificates be attested
1587 by some external entity (a certification authority, the Certificate Transparency log, etc.).

1588 **Retrieving the certificate(s).**   The beacon must make available online the current cer-
1589 tificate and all previous certificates, so that it is always possible to verify signatures and
1590 certificates of old pulses. This is handled by interface call 3g defined in Section 6.4.

1591 ## 4.9   The Output Value

1592 **Field name:**   `outputValue` or (abbreviated) `randOut`

1593 **Default type:** hashOut

1594 **Relations:** $F_{21,i} = \texttt{randOut}_i = \left(\texttt{hash}\left(\|_{k\in\{1,\ldots,120\}}\overline{F_{k,i}}\right)\right)$, that is:

$$Z \leftarrow \texttt{Byt\_serialize\_fields}(\langle \texttt{uri}, \texttt{version},$$
$$\texttt{cipher}, \texttt{period}, \texttt{certId}, \texttt{chainId}, \texttt{pulseId}, \texttt{time},$$
$$\texttt{randLocal}, \texttt{ext.srcId}, \texttt{ext.status}, \texttt{ext.value},$$
$$\texttt{previous}, \texttt{hour}, \texttt{day}, \texttt{month}, \texttt{year}, \texttt{preCom}, \texttt{status}, \texttt{sig}\rangle) \quad (17)$$
$$\texttt{randOut} \leftarrow \texttt{hash}(Z) \quad (18)$$

1595 **Description:** The value in the `randOut` field is called the *output value* of the pulse. It is
1596 the `hash()` of the values in all previous fields of the pulse. This accomplishes several goals:

1597 1. Since it hashes `preCom`, which in turn is the hash of a fresh `randLocal` (to be released
1598 only in the next pulse), it contains fresh (and approximately) full entropy.

1599 2. Even if a malicious Beacon operator controls any other field (e.g., `preCom`,
1600 `ext.srcId`, `ext.value`), controlling n bits of `randOut` would require computational
1601 effort exponential in n.

1602 3. A sequence of consecutive pulses constitutes a hash chain, which means each pulse
1603 with a latest timestamp commits all previous pulses.

1604 **Guidance:** User applications relying on a single Beacon **SHALL** use `randOut`, rather than
1605 `randLocal`, as the public randomness output of the Beacon (see Section 7 for details).

5 | Hash Chains and the Skip List

1606

1607 Each pulse contains an `outputValue` field, which is the hash of all the other fields in the
1608 pulse. Each pulse also contains a `previous` field, which contains the `outputValue` of the
1609 previous pulse. Putting these two fields together, a sequence of pulses makes up a *hash*
1610 *chain*. A hash chain ensures that **once a single pulse is known, previous pulses CANNOT**
1611 **be changed** without leaving obvious evidence in the chain.

5.1 Hash Chains
1612

1613 A sequence of consecutive pulses makes up a hash chain, as shown in Fig. 6. The Figure
1614 also illustrates the relation between three fields in consecutive pulse:

1615   • `timeStamp` — incremented by 1 minute in each pulse.

1616   • `previous` — a copy of the `outputValue` field from the previous pulse.

1617   • `outputValue` — the hash() of all other fields in its pulse.

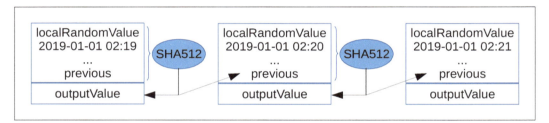

Figure 6. The sequence of pulses forms a hash chain

1618   In order to make these diagrams legible, most pulse fields are omitted, some fieldnames
1619 are shortened, and `timeStamp` values are in the **yyyy-mm-dd hh:mm** (RFC3339) format.
1620 All examples in this document assume that the beacon is producing pulses once per minute.

1621   The important security property of a hash chain is that **changing any record requires**
1622 **changing all future records.** That is, if we alter any field in a given pulse, this must
1623 change its `outputValue`, since that value is the hash of the other fields of the pulse. That
1624 `outputValue` is then included in the next pulse. A changed value there must lead to a
1625 changed value in the `outputValue` of the next *next* pulse. And so on — any change to
1626 a pulse propagates forward forever. Figure 7 shows an example of how this works. This
1627 property implies that, as long as beacon pulses are widely seen and recorded, it is impossible
1628 for even the beacon operator to alter a past pulse without detection.

5.2 Skiplists
1629

1630 Section 5.1 showed that, by verification of the hash-chain created across consecutive pulses,
1631 anyone who has recorded the pulse at time *T* CAN later review any previous pulse at time

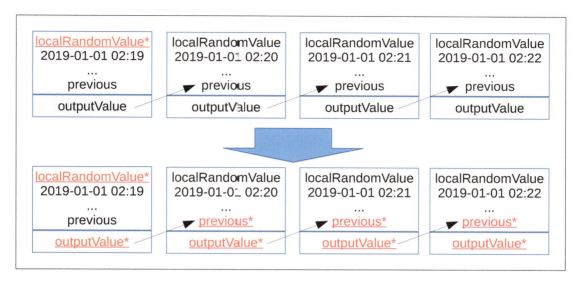

Figure 7. A change in one pulse propagates to all later ones via the hash chain

1632 $T - K$, and verify that the latter has not been changed. However, checking the chain across
1633   every consecutive pulse requires examining *every pulse* from time $T - K$ through time T,
1634   as illustrated in Fig. 8a. Using this approach, verifying that a pulse from one year ago is
1635   consistent with the most recent pulse requires examining over *half a million* pulses, which
1636   can be unworkably long. A security mechanism that is impractically inefficient will seldom
1637   be used. The solution to this problem is a *skiplist*.

1638   Consider that a user of the beacon starts out knowing the value of one pulse (the
1639   ANCHOR), from 2022-10-04 17:35 The user wants to verify that the value of a much
1640   earlier pulse (the TARGET), at 2019-11-29 22:08, is consistent with the later (ANCHOR)
1641   pulse. The user thus contacts the beacon frontend and requests a skiplist from the beacon.
1642   The beacon responds with a short sequence of pulses constituting an intact hash chain from
1643   TARGET to ANCHOR.

1644   Why is it possible to construct a short intact hash chain between such distant pulses?
1645   Because of the additional linking fields added in version 2.0.0, namely year, month, day,
1646   and hour. These ensure that there are *many different* hash chains, of many different lengths,
1647   running through the sequence of pulses.

1648   The existence of all these linking fields (year, month, day, hour, as well as previous),
1649   and all the corresponding combinations of hash chains, means that, between a given
1650   TARGET and ANCHOR, there are in general *many* different pulse sequences that contain
1651   an intact hash chain. Algorithm 5 gives a procedure for selecting a minimal-length chain.
1652   The same algorithm is illustrated in Fig. 8b.

1653   Figure 8 compares, side by side, the case of a complete hash-chain (in Fig. 8a) vs.

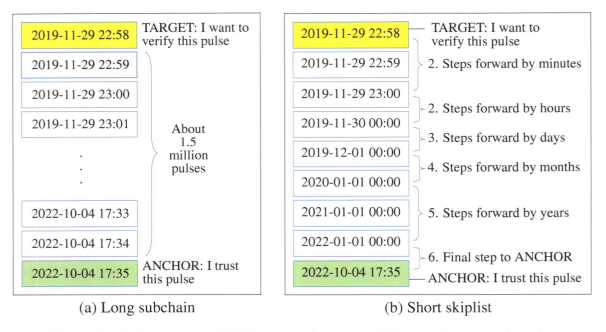

(a) Long subchain   (b) Short skiplist

Figure 8. Linking a trusted ANCHOR pulse to a TARGET pulse for verification

the case of a corresponding skiplist (in Fig. 8b). The efficiency improvement brought by the skiplist is huge: from about 1.5 million pulses to 9 pulses. However, this example was chosen to provide a relatively short skiplist, for ease of explanation. In general, for TARGET and ANCHOR points Y years apart (each on a uniformly random minute, hour and day of the corresponding year), we expect a skiplist to be about $Y + 62$ pulses long. On average we need to obtain, besides the TARGET and the ANCHOR, about 28.5 pulses that are not first-in-an-hour, 11.5 first-in-an-hour pulses that are not first-in-a-day, 14.5 first-in-a-day pulses that are not first-in-a-month , 5.5 first-in-a-month pulses that are not first-in-a-year, and Y first-in-a-year pulses.

To verify the performance of the skiplists in the general case, we randomly selected TARGET and ANCHOR points which were different time-intervals apart: one day, 30 days, one year, and ten years. For each duration, we repeated the experiment 100,000 times, and found the shortest, average, and longest skiplists from all our experiments. The results are summarized in Table 7.

Table 7. Length of skiplists (in pulses), by duration

Time interval	Minimum	Average	Maximum
1 day	2	43.2	84
30 days	2	57.8	113
1 year	3	63.2	124
10 years	12	72.1	132

Algorithm 5 Construct a skiplist from TARGET to ANCHOR.

1: **function** MAKE_SKIPLIST(TARGET, ANCHOR)
2:     path ← []
3:     current ← TARGET
4:     **while** current< ANCHOR **do**
5:         path ← pp ‖current
6:         **if** current is first pulse in its **year then**
7:             current ← first pulse in NEXT **year**
8:         **else if** current is first pulse in its **month then**
9:             current ← first pulse in NEXT **month**
10:         **else if** current is first pulse in its **day then**
11:             current ← first pulse in NEXT **day**
12:         **else if** current is first pulse in its **hour then**
13:             current ← first pulse in NEXT **hour**
14:         **else**
15:             current ← NEXT pulse
16:     path ← path ‖ANCHOR
17:     **return** (path)

5.3 Verifying a Skiplist

The new beacon frontend supports requests for skiplists — when asked, it will produce a skiplist that provides an intact hash chain between a requested TARGET and ANCHOR value. The skiplists are short and efficient to construct, so supporting such requests imposes little burden on the frontend (web server).

Similarly, verifying a skiplist is very efficient. The requirement for a skiplist to be valid is simple: *each pulse in the skiplist must contain the* outputValue *field of the previous pulse in one of its linking fields (that is,* year, month, day, hour, *or* previous*). We provide a procedure for verifying that a skiplist gives an intact hash chain in Algorithm 6.

Algorithm 6 Verify a skiplist from TARGET to ANCHOR.

1: **function** VERIFY_SKIPLIST(TARGET, ANCHOR, path)
2:     n ← number of entries in path. // path *is indexed from 1 to n*
3:     Q ← path[1]
4:     **for** i ← 2...n **do**
5:         current ← path[i]
6:         **if** $Q.out \notin$ current.{year, month, day, hour, previous} **then**
7:             **return** False
8:     **return** True

1677 | **6   The Beacon Interface**

1678 This section describes the interface that a beacon frontend SHOULD support for retrieval
1679 requests (a.k.a. calls or queries) by users. The Beacon Engine is not involved in the handling
1680 of queries, since it SHOULD be isolated as much as possible. Instead, queries received via
1681 a web-interface (frontend) are processed as queries to the external database of the Beacon.
1682 The section describes first a general syntax for queries (Section 6.1) and then the mandatory
1683 and optional queries. The calls are organized according to the type of requested data:
1684 individual pulses (Section 6.2), sequences of pulses (Section 6.3), related to certificates
1685 (Section 6.4), related to external values (Section 6.5), and related to local functioning
1686 (Section 6.6). The calls identified as optional MAY be changed, deprecated or promoted
1687 to mandatory in future sub-versions (2.0.z) or versions (2.y.z) of the Beacon Reference.

1688 6.1   General syntax for queries and replies

1689 A deployed Beacon SHOULD use an *application programming interface* (API) based on
1690 *representational state transfer* (REST) calls conveyed through URIs. Queries are trans-
1691 formed into GET operations, then resulting in a reply in some expected language/format. It
1692 is intended that users CAN use a regular web-browser to query a beacon.

1693 6.1.1   General query-format

1694 Any query must be specifiable via an appropriate URI that contains as prefix a URL that
1695 identifies the beacon. This URL prefix, denoted hereafter as ⟨*beaconURL*⟩, is not a field
1696 of the pulse format but is a prefix of the value in the `uri` value of the most recent pulses.
1697 Recalling the definitions in §4.2.1, the value ⟨*beaconURL*⟩ CAN be described as:

$$\langle beaconURL\rangle = \langle webPrefix{:}\text{str}\rangle/\texttt{beacon}/\langle version{:}\text{str}\rangle. \tag{19}$$

1698 For example, this value is https://beacon.nist.gov/beacon/2.0 in the current NIST beacon.

1699   The full URI is composed of the mentioned prefix and additional elements that specify
1700 the parameters of the query. These additional elements MAY for example include timestamp
1701 values, or pulse and chain indices. Each query indicates a type of intended response, such as a
1702 single pulse (§6.2), or a sequence of pulses (§6.3). There are also queries for associated data,
1703 such as for an X.509 certificate (§6.4), or for the text that describes an external source (§6.5).

1704 6.1.2   General reply-format

1705 Possible reply formats include *bare* (a simple concatenation of byte-serialized fields, similar
1706 to what was described in Section 4.1.3), *txt* (a MIME type text/plain document, assembled

1707   in a .txt file with UTF8 encoding), *hypertext markup language* (HTML), *javascript object*
1708   *notation* (JSON), and *extensible markup language* (XML).

1709   This document defined the *bare* and *txt* formats. The specification of the remaining
1710   formats is currently deferred to a future external document.

1711   The reply format **MAY** either be implicitly decided by the Beacon or explicitly specified
1712   by the user when making a query. For the latter, the user appends to the query URI the string
1713   "?format=⟨*format*⟩", where ⟨*format*⟩ is a short identifier of the intended format, e.g., bare,
1714   html, json, txt, xml. For example, a URI ending with "?format=xml" will specify a query
1715   whose output **SHOULD** be produced with an XML format.

1716   **Mandatory support.** In the current beacon reference version (2.0.0), a beacon is only re-
1717   quired to satisfy at least one of the above mentioned formats. Future reference updates (2.0.z
1718   and 2.y.z) **MAY** require that the support for some specific formats becomes mandatory. Sec-
1719   tion 6.6 specifies an optional (recommended) query (5j) whose reply enumerates/describes
1720   the types of format supported by the Beacon for each type of query.

1721   When a reply format is specified explicitly, the reply **SHOULD** enable saving the output
1722   as a file with a name extension (.txt, .json, .xml, ...) that identifies the format.

1723   **Remark on types of format.** Fieldnames are not part of the content of a pulse, and so do
1724   not appear in the bare format. However, some reply formats (e.g., xml) contain a structure
1725   that labels each field value with is a corresponding field name. This motivates distinguishing
1726   two types of reply format:

1727   • **Untagged.** Some formats contain an implicit structure that is not obvious from the
1728   output alone and does not explicitly identify the type of included components. For
1729   example, in the case of replies containing a pulse, this happens with the *bare* and the
1730   *bare-txt* formats, similar to what was described in Section 4.1.3. Those formats do
1731   not specify any fieldname, and instead consist simply of a concatenation of serialized
1732   field values, in an expected order and length.

1733   • **Tagged.** Some formats contain a structure of tags that enable explicit identification of
1734   the type of content. For example, in the case of replies containing a pulse, the reply
1735   will contain tags that identify each field by fieldname. This intends to make easier the
1736   parsing and consistency checking of of values of each field of a pulse.

1737   **Error responses.** Each of the described calls returns either a suitable reply, when one
1738   exists, or an error message.

1739 **6.2 Queries for single pulses**

1740 Table 8 enumerates the mandatory calls for single pulses, showing their designations and
1741 the corresponding URIs. Each of the described queries returns either a suitable pulse (if one
1742 exists) or else a 404 error message.

Table 8. Interface calls for individual pulses

#	Designation	URI
1p	Pulse $\langle pid$:dec$\rangle$ in Chain $\langle cid$:dec$\rangle$	$\langle beaconURL\rangle$/chain/$\langle cid$:dec$\rangle$/pulse/$\langle pid$:dec$\rangle$
1q	Pulse at Time GEQ to $\langle ts$:str$\rangle$	$\langle beaconURL\rangle$/pulse/time/$\langle ts$:str$\rangle$
1r	Pulse at Time Previous to $\langle ts$:str$\rangle$	$\langle beaconURL\rangle$/pulse/time/previous/$\langle ts$:str$\rangle$
1s	Pulse at Time Next to $\langle ts$:str$\rangle$	$\langle beaconURL\rangle$/pulse/time/next/$\langle ts$:str$\rangle$
1t	Latest Pulse	$\langle beaconURL\rangle$/pulse/last

1743   Below follows a description of the output of each call:

1744 **1p. Pulse $\langle pid$:dec$\rangle$ in Chain $\langle cid$:dec$\rangle$.** Returns, from within the chain with index
1745 $\langle cid$:dec$\rangle$ (or, if $\langle cid$:dec$\rangle$=last, from the chain with maximal index), the pulse P
1746   that has pulse index P.pulseIndex=$\langle pid$:dec$\rangle$ (or, if $\langle pid$:dec$\rangle$=last, the pulse with
1747   maximal pulse index). Although the fields $\langle pid$:dec$\rangle$ and $\langle cid$:dec$\rangle$ are here described
1748   as requiring decimal format, they **MAY** also be filled with the four-character string
1749   "last" to denote a query for the corresponding largest produced value(s) (of chainId
1750   and/or pulseId, respectively).

1751 **1q. Pulse at Time GEQ to $\langle ts$:str$\rangle$.** Returns the pulse that has the smallest time value
1752   *greater or equal* (GEQ) to the timestamp specified by $\langle ts$:str$\rangle$. Particularly: if there
1753   is a pulse P satisfying P.time=$\langle ts$:str$\rangle$, then that pulse is returned; otherwise the pulse
1754   with smaller $\langle ts'\rangle$=P.time satisfying $\langle ts'\rangle > \langle ts\rangle$ is returned, if one exists.

1755 **1r. Pulse at Time Previous to $\langle ts$:str$\rangle$.** Returns the pulse that has the larger time value
1756   that is smaller than the time specified by $\langle ts$:str$\rangle$.

1757 **1s. Pulse at Time Next to $\langle ts$:str$\rangle$.** Returns the pulse that has the smaller time value
1758   that is larger than $\langle ts$:str$\rangle$.

1759 **1t. Latest Pulse.** Returns the last available pulse on the last chain, i.e., the pulse $P_{j,i}$
1760   satisfying P.chainId $= j$ and P.pulseId $= i$, such that there is no other pulse
1761   with larger chain index (in chainId), and such that within the chain with index
1762 j there is no pulse with pulse index (in pulseId) larger than i. Note that this
1763   query is an abbreviation of what **CAN** also be obtained with the query 1p, as
1764 $\langle beaconURL\rangle$/chain/last/pulse/last

1765 **6.3 Queries for sequences of pulses**

1766 Table 9 enumerates the mandatory calls for sequences of pulses. The currently defined
1767 sequences are skiplists and subchains. Each of the described queries returns either a suitable
1768 non-empty sequence of pulse (if one exists) or else a 404 error message.

Table 9. Interface call for sequences (skiplists and subchains) of pulses

#	Designation	URI	Opt?
2m	Skiplist between Times $\langle ts_1$:str$\rangle$ and $\langle ts_2$:str$\rangle$	$\langle beaconURL\rangle$/skiplist/time/$\langle ts_1$:str$\rangle$/ $\langle ts_2$:str$\rangle$	
2n	Skiplist in Chain $\langle cid\rangle$ between Pulses $\langle pid_1$:dec$\rangle$ and $\langle pid_2$:dec$\rangle$	$\langle beaconURL\rangle$/skiplist/chain/$\langle cid$:dec$\rangle$/ pulse/$\langle pid_1$:dec$\rangle$/$\langle pid_2$:dec$\rangle$	
2o	Subchain across Times $\langle ts_1$:str$\rangle$ and $\langle ts_2$:str$\rangle$	$\langle beaconURL\rangle$/subchain/time/$\langle ts_1$:str$\rangle$/ $\langle ts_2$:str$\rangle$	yes
2p	Subchain of Chain $\langle cid$:dec$\rangle$ across Pulses $\langle pid_1$:dec$\rangle$ and $\langle pid_2$:dec$\rangle$	$\langle beaconURL\rangle$/subchain/chain/$\langle cid$:dec$\rangle$/ pulse/$\langle pid_1$:dec$\rangle$/$\langle pid_2$:dec$\rangle$	yes

"Opt?=yes" means that the support is optional (i.e., not mandatory).

1769 **2m. Skiplist between Times $\langle ts_1$:str$\rangle$ and $\langle ts_2$:str$\rangle$.** Returns a sequence of pulses, in
1770   ascending chronological order of the value in the `timeStamp` field, and such that:

1771   i) the first pulse in the sequence has timestamp exactly $\langle ts_1$:str$\rangle$;

1772   ii) any pair (P,P') of consecutive pulses in the sequence satisfies P.`randOut` =
1773 $P'.\langle field\rangle$, for some $\langle field\rangle$ in {`out.Prev, out.H, out.D, out.M, out.Y`};

1774   iii) the last pulse in the sequence has timestamp exactly $\langle ts_2$:str$\rangle$.

1775 **2n. Skiplist in Chain $\langle cid\rangle$ across Pulses $\langle pid_1\rangle$ and $\langle pid_2\rangle$.** Reply is similar to the case
1776   of query 2m ("Skiplist between Times $\langle ts_1\rangle$ and $\langle ts_2\rangle$"), but the anchor and target
1777   pulses in the query are instead defined by pulse indices (in `pulseId`), within the scope
1778   of a particular chain index (in `chainId`).

1779 **2o. Subchain across Times $\langle ts_1$:str$\rangle$ and $\langle ts_2$:str$\rangle$.** Similar to call 2m ("Skiplist between
1780   Times") but changing condition ii) as follows: "any pair (P,P') of consecutive pulses
1781   in the sequence satisfies P.`randOut` $= P'$.`previous`.

1782 **2p. Subchain of Chain, across Pulses $\langle pid_1$:dec$\rangle$ and $\langle pid_1$:dec$\rangle$.** This is a dual of the
1783   call 2o ("Subchain across Times"). The reply is similar to that of the call 2n ("Skiplist
1784   in Chain, across between Pulses"), but changing condition ii) as follows: "any pair
1785 (P,P') of consecutive pulses in the sequence satisfied P.`randOut` $= P'$.`previous`.

1786 **6.4 Queries associated with certificates**

1787 Table 10 enumerates queries related to certificates.

49

Table 10. Interface calls for associated data

#	Designation	URI	Opt?
3g	Certificate with ID ⟨*certId*:hex⟩	⟨*beaconURL*⟩/certificate/⟨*certId*:hex⟩	
3h	List certIDs in Chain ⟨*cid*:dec⟩	⟨*beaconURL*⟩/listCertIds/chain/⟨*cid*:dec⟩	yes

1788   **3g**. **Certificate with ID ⟨*certId*:hex⟩.** Returns a Base 64 encoded RFC 5280 PKIX
1789   Certficate (PEM Format) file whose `hash()` is equal to ⟨*certId*:hex⟩.

1790   **3h**. **List certIDs in Chain ⟨*cid*⟩.** Returns a list of all distinct `certId` values used by the
1791   Beacon in the chain(s) with `certId` indicated by ⟨*cid*⟩. Using ⟨*cid*⟩="All" indicates
1792   that the reply **SHOULD** cover all values `certId` used across all chains. For each
1793   distinct `certId`, it also shows the values `version`, `cipher`, `chainId`, `pulseId` and
1794   `time`, of the pulses where the corresponding `certId` was first used and/or when the
1795   previous pulse had a different certificate. Thus, the reply is actually a list of sixtets.

1796 **6.5 Queries associated with external values**

1797   Table 11 enumerates calls related to external values.

Table 11. Interface calls related to usage of external values

#	Designation	URI	Opt?
4m	External Source Description with Identifier ⟨*extSrcId*:hex⟩	⟨*beaconURL*⟩/extSrcId/⟨*extSrcId*:hex⟩	
4n	Pre-image of extSource ⟨*extValue*:hex⟩	⟨*beaconURL*⟩/extValue/⟨*extValue*:hex⟩	yes
4o	List first PulseIds for all extValues with Source Identifier ⟨*extSrcId*:hex⟩	⟨*beaconURL*⟩/listPulseIds/extSrcId/ ⟨*extSrcId*:hex⟩	yes
4p	Range of PulseIds in Chain ⟨*cid*:dec⟩ using extValue ⟨*extValue*:hex⟩	⟨*beaconURL*⟩/listPulseIds/chain/ ⟨*cid*:dec⟩/extValue/⟨*extValue*:hex⟩	yes

1798   **4m**. **External Source Description with Identifier ⟨*extSrcId*:hex⟩.** Returns a MIME
1799   type text/plain document whose `hash()` is (in hexadecimal format) ⟨*extSrcId*:hex⟩.
1800   The document contains a description of an external source and provides guidance
1801   to when and how to include content generated therefrom. The content generated
1802   in that form, from time to time, is the one whose `hash()` is to be placed in the field
1803   `external.value` of some pulses. If the beacon does not recognize ⟨*extSrcId*:hex⟩
1804   as a used `ext.srcId`, then it returns a 404 error.

1805   **4n**. **Pre-image of extSourceValue ⟨*extValue*:hex⟩.** Returns the content whose `hash()` is,
1806   in hexadecimal format, the value ⟨*extValue*:hex⟩ that is used in the field `ext.value`
1807   of some pulse produced by the Beacon. If ⟨*extValue*:hex⟩ is the all-zeros string (64
1808   hexa-decimal characters "0" if the used `hash()` has 512 bits of output), then the

1809   reply is a message explaining that the all-zeros string is the default value when an
1810   external source has not been used in some chain. If the Beacon does not recognize
1811   the provided $\langle extValue\text{:hex}\rangle$, then it returns a 404 error response.

1812   **4o. List first PulseId for all extValues with Identifier $\langle extSrcId\text{:hex}\rangle$.** Returns a
1813   list of triplets $\langle$`chainId`, `pulseId`, `time`$\rangle$ of the first pulses that have used each
1814   external-source value corresponding to the identifier $\langle extSrcId\text{:hex}\rangle$.

1815   **4p. Range of PulseIds in Chain $\langle cid\text{:dec}\rangle$ using extValue $\langle extValue\text{:hex}\rangle$.** Returns an
1816   abbreviated list (range) of the `pulseId` indices of all pulses, within chain $\langle cid\text{:dec}\rangle$,
1817   than have the value $\langle extValue\text{:hex}\rangle$ in the field `ext.value`. The elements of the
1818   abbreviated list are written succinctly as ranges, where for example $p_1 : p_2$ denotes
1819   the sequence $p_1, p_1 + 1, ..., p_2$.

1820   6.6   Queries about local functioning

1821   Table 12 enumerates calls related to local properties of the Beacon functioning.

Table 12. Queries about local properties of the Beacon

#	Designation	URI	Opt?
5j	Supported queries	$\langle beaconURL\rangle$/queries	yes
5k	Local status flags	$\langle beaconURL\rangle$/status/flags	yes
5l	Local history	$\langle beaconURL\rangle$/history/	yes

1822   **5j. Supported queries.** Returns a structured description of the supported queries, ex-
1823   plaining for each the syntax of the URI query and the default and supported reply
1824   formats (containing some non-empty subset of {bare, bare-txt, html, json, xml}).

1825   **5k. Local status flags.** Returns a MIME type text/plain document containing a human
1826   readable description of the defined bit flags of the `statusCode` field. The output is a
1827   file named "beacon-status-flags.txt" Each new line is of the form: "Flag #n (the nth
1828   LSB of the `statusCode` field): additive value equal to 2^n: set (1) if $\langle describe\ if\ 1\rangle$;
1829   unset (0) if $\langle describe\ if\ 0\rangle$." In this description, n is to be replaced by a corresponding
1830   integer between 1 and 32.

1831   **5l. Local history.** Returns a MIME type text/plain document containing a human read-
1832   able description of relevant information about the local functioning of the Beacon.
1833   This MAY include anything deemed useful by the Beacon operator, including an
1834   explanation about past or planned outages, existing time-gaps, chain terminations,
1835   external repositories storing past pulses.

1836 **7 Using a Beacon**

1837 A beacon is useful in many situations. For example:

1838   1. When multiple parties want to coordinate some action based on a random number, but
1839   do not want any one among them to be able to exert control over the random number.

1840   2. When someone wants proof that some computation could not have been started before
1841   a particular time T.

1842   3. When one party wants to demonstrate to the world (including many people who will
1843   only become interested much later) having carried out some random process fairly,
1844   without "cooking" random numbers.

1845   4. When multiple parties want to run some cryptographic protocol based on a shared
1846   random string, but do not want the added communications overhead of establishing a
1847   shared random string.

1848   In this section, we discuss useful techniques for using a beacon intelligently. This is sim-
1849 ply an attempt to provide a cookbook for people who are not cryptographers, but would like
1850 to know how to use a beacon. It may also act as a kind of Schelling point, helping different
1851 people to efficiently coordinate on doing things the same way without a lot of negotiation.

1852 **7.1   Direct usage — sampling a single integer using the modulo technique**

1853 When a single random integer is needed, it CAN be extracted very simply from the field
1854 randOut of a single pulse, by using the *modulo technique*. If the integer is to be sampled
1855 from within the range $Range = [0, N-1]$, with the number of bits of N being significantly
1856 smaller than the number of bits (512) in randOut, then an application CAN use

$$\text{randOut} \bmod (N). \tag{20}$$

1857 The application software needs to support arithmetic with precision large enough to handle
1858 the 512 bits of the randOut field (a hash output).

1859   To sample an integer from a more general range $Range = [L, L+N-1]$, where L is
1860 any non-negative integer, and N is limited as before, the application CAN compute

$$L + (\text{randOut} \bmod (N)). \tag{21}$$

1861   As hinted above, the suitability of the modulo technique is conditioned to a limitation
1862 on the size of N, as compared to 2^{512}. This relates to the *distribution bias* (e.g., see
1863 Ref. [NIS13b]) induced by taking the modulo, when N is not a power of 2.

1864   As a simple rule, to ensure that the bias is negligible, we recommend that the modulo
1865 technique be used only if N is not greater than 2^{384}. This guarantees a bias smaller than

1866 2^{-128} (i.e., under the working assumption that the hash output `randOut` is uniformly
1867 random in $[0, 2^{512} - 1]$). Exceptionally, the technique CAN also be used if N is an exact
1868 power of two, not larger than 2^{512}, since then the modulo does not produce bias.

1869   Section 7.3 discusses the case where the range is of width larger than 2^{512}, or when more
1870 than one random number is required.

7.2 Ex post facto-verifiable random sampling

1871

1872 Random sampling is used extensively in industry, research, and activities like lotteries. After
1873 the sampling has been done, it may be hard to convince a distrusting third person that the
1874 sampling was indeed random. In this section we discuss how this CAN be achieved using a
1875 public source of randomness.

1876   In order to conduct random sampling that is ex post facto-verifiable, the user must first
1877 derive a seed, Z, from the output of the beacon. The seed needs to be derived in a way that
1878 includes all relevant information. Often, it will be worthwhile to cryptographically bind
1879 some particular information into the seed. That seed MAY then be used to generate a longer
1880 sequence of pseudorandom output bits, or to select some value from a set of possible values.

1881   We CAN thus split the process of using the beacon outputs into three phases:

1882 1. **commit upfront** — commit upfront, before the time of the required beacon pulse(s),
1883   to how the seed will be obtained and what will be done with the seed;

1884 2. **derive a seed** — receive the intended pulses and derive a seed from them;

1885 3. **use the seed** — use the seed to do something previously committed to.

7.2.1 Committing upfront

1886

1887 An essential principle for secure use of beacon randomness is that **everything about the**
1888 **use of the future random number from the beacon needs to be specified in advance.**

1889 **High-level example.**   If a user plans to use the beacon to select a subset of polling places
1890 to audit from an election, the user needs to specify, in advance:

1891 1. Which beacon will be used, e.g., by specifying the administrative domain, e.g., spec-
1892   ified with the help of the *webPrefix* sub-field included in the `uri` (see Section 4.2.1).

1893 2. Which beacon pulse (specifying the `chainId` and `time`) will be used (assuming the
1894   chain remains active and without gaps including the intended timestamp and vicinity).

1895 3. The set of polling places and how many of them will be selected.

1896 4. The program for using a seed to select a subset of polling places for audits.

1897
1898
5. How to handle exceptional conditions, e.g., if the beacon fails to produce a pulse at the specified time (due to a time gap), or if the chain ends before the intended time.

1899 **Procedure.**   In order to make the commitment clear, we recommend the following steps:

1900
1901
1. Write a single program, *Prog*, which will take as input a seed Z to be obtained from the beacon pulse(s) used, and which will produce the desired output from this step.

1902
2. Write a *committing statement M*, containing:

1903
1904
1905
(a) A text, M_1, explaining how the seed Z is to be constructed from a beacon pulse (and which pulse) and from the hash H (not yet computed) of the committing statement M. For Example:

1906
```
The seed Z shall be obtained as the SHA512 hash of the
concatenation of:  the SHA512 hash (H) of the committing
statement M; and the randOut value (P[T].randOut)
of the NIST Beacon pulse with timestamp T equal to
2018-07-04 12:00:00.000.
```

1907
(b) The hash() (in hex string representation) of the program *Prog*.

1908
(c) A text, M_3, describing what will be done with the outputs of *Prog*. For example:

1909
```
Each of the 16 outputs is the number of a precinct to be
audited by hand.
```

1910
1911
(d) A text, M_4, that indexes (order and file name) and explains the content of the auxiliary documents needed to specify what is happening. For example:

1912
```
File #1, named precincts.pdf, with 372,824 bytes, contains
the precinct map that labels each precinct and its polling
place.  File #2, named voters.ods, with 142,193 bytes,
contains a spreadsheet with the number of registered voters
per polling place.
```

1913
1914
(e) A text, M_5, that describes the hash() (as hex strings) of each of the auxiliary files, in the same order they are described. For example:

1915
```
The auxiliary files have the following SHA512 hashes:  File
#1 --- efda3b6628211e02 aba9cdae11fcff5f 34550211f54558ef fd13687ab204e4db
5b9121332e5931c8 564bc858ec9545bd 8dc81d9da5b2eaa3 7e7e9bf251307dc7; File
#2 --- 27881a1d15e0df72 cbc4aa8ed393dbd4 7de5b6fde72d8cfe 0e9da389af1e6c7c
c95089c7bdc52c38 cee79bb3473a90e8 2fb96968b9978700 b7438e53b9059797.
```

1916
1917
1918
3. Commit in public to $H = \text{hash}(Prog \parallel M)$. Optionally, one CAN also publish immediately the actual program *Prog* and committing statement M. Nonetheless, they are both already committed by the hash H.

1919
1920
4. When the intended beacon pulse ($P[T]$) becomes available, derive the seed Z as described and use it as the input to the program *Prog*.

1921   5. Report the results of the program.

1922 **Requirement:** *A program that will run based on a future beacon pulse must be entirely*
1923 *deterministic, given the beacon pulse and other inputs.*

1924   Although a committing statement M SHOULD be published before the timestamp of the
1925 pulse being used to generate the seed, it is important to have a clearly defined committing
1926 statement, even if not published ahead of time.

1927   When the committing statement will not be published ahead of time, it is specially
1928 important that a "distinguished" (i.e., default) timestamp be used, to mitigate the possibility
1929 (or appearance) that someone might try many timestamps until they found one that fits their
1930 purposes unusually well. That is

1931   1. On each day, the default timestamp to use is yyyy-mm-dd 12:00:00.000.

1932   2. On each month, the default timestamp to use is yyyy-mm-01 12:00:00.000.

1933   If a specific reason justifies using a different timestamp, such as
1934 2018-09-13 17:35:00.000, that reason SHOULD be explained ahead of time by the
1935 user of the beacon. (An example of a good reason would be some predetermined schedule
1936 for using the beacon pulse, which needed to start immediately after 17:35.)

1937   When a committing statement is not being published before the pulse to be used, the
1938 user SHOULD choose the timestamp with UTC of noon (yyyy-mm-dd 12:00:00.000) on a
1939 day, and if possible SHOULD use the one on the first of the month. If the committing
1940 statement is published or committed to in public (by revealing H, for example) at least
1941 a day in advance, then this is not necessary. However, users of the beacon SHOULD use
1942 these distinguished/default timestamps whenever possible, and SHOULD explain any other
1943 choices made. (For example, if some auditing process must start promptly at 10:14 PM local
1944 time, that would be a good reason to use a different pulse.)

1945 **7.2.2 Deriving a Seed**

1946 The simplest way to derive a seed, which is appropriate in almost all cases, is to hash
1947 together a committing statement with the randOut of the beacon pulse described in the
1948 committing statement. Thus, if we have a committing statement that says we will use the
1949 pulse at 2019-02-22 12:00, then we compute the seed as

$$H \leftarrow \text{hash}(\text{committing statement referencing NIST beacon pulse at 2019-02-22 12:00})$$
$$Z \leftarrow \text{hash}(H \parallel P[\text{2018-07-04 12:00}].\text{randOut})$$

1950   Recall that the randOut field is the hash() of all other fields in the beacon pulse. This
1951 limits the ability of even a crooked or subverted beacon to exert control over the results.

1952 **7.3 Using the Seed**

1953 When a seed Z needs to be used to generate a very long output string, such as might be used
1954 for many different individual outputs, we recommend the procedure based on Algorithm 7.

Algorithm 7 Generate distinct values from a short seed.

1: **function** EXPAND(Z, i)
2:    $V \leftarrow \text{hash}(0x00 \parallel Z)$
3:    **return** $(\text{hash}(0x01 \parallel V \parallel \text{encode\_uint}(i, 64)))$

1955   For each new index i, Algorithm 7 outputs a new distinct output $Y_i = \text{EXPAND}(Z, i)$,
1956 with n bits (the bit-length of the output of $\text{hash}()$). Thus, by incrementing the index i, the
1957 function **CAN** be used to generate, from a single seed Z, as many pseudo-random n-bit
1958 values as desired.

1959   If the range of output values needed is within $[A, \dots, B-1]$ and if $\log_2(B-A) \le n - 128$,
1960 then each value **CAN** be mapped into a *result* in that range, with a bias less that 2^{-128}, as:

$$\text{result} \leftarrow A + (Y_i \ (\text{mod} \ B - A)) \tag{22}$$

1961 **7.4 Combining Beacons**

1962 The `preCom` and `randLocal` fields are used to derive a seed from a combination of beacons.
1963 The procedure also uses the field `randOut`, in order to achieve security against misbehavior
1964 by one of the beacons.

1965   The procedure specification requires identifying the involved beacons, e.g., A and
1966 B (preferably administratively independent) and the future sampling timing T. These
1967 parameters are described in a (committing) statement M and then the statement is hashed
1968 into a commitment $H = \text{hash}(M)$ of the procedure.

1969   The process is then as follows (exemplified for the case of only two beacons operating
1970 on the same pulsating schedule):

1971 1. Within the time window T and $T + 3\pi/4$, sample pulses $A[T]$ and $B[T]$ and check their
1972   standalone correctness. If any of $P_A[T]$ and $P_B[T]$ is not obtained until time $T + 3\pi/4$,
1973   or if any of them is *invalid*, then abort this attempt to combine beacon pulses, else
1974   continue. The notion of valid vs. invalid needs to be unambiguously identified by
1975   the user application. In any case, the case of a gap or lost `randLocal` in any of the
1976   required pulses of any of the Beacons (A and B) **SHOULD** invalidate the combination.

1977   Note: Since Promise 1 requires beacons to not release the next pulse before $T + \pi$,
1978   the sampling window ensures that the user either gives up or learns $A[T].\text{preCom}$ and
1979 $B[T].\text{preCom}$ before anyone knows $A[T + \pi].\text{randLocal}$ and $B[T + \pi].\text{randLocal}$.

2. Within the time window $T + \pi$ and $T + 2\pi$, sample pulses $P_A[T + \pi]$ and $P_B[T + \pi]$ and check their standalone correctness. If any of $P_A[T]$ and $P_B[T]$ is not obtained until time $T + 2\pi$, or if any of them is invalid, then abort this attempt to combine beacon pulses, else continue.

3. If for any Beacon the 1st bit-flag of statusCode$[T + \pi]$ is set to 1 (indicating that exceptionally randLocal is not a pre-image of the previous preCom), i.e., if $d[T + \pi]$.statusCode$\&1 = 1$ for any $d \in \{A, B\}$, then abort this attempt to combine beacon pulses, else continue.

4. Verify that $P_d[T]$.preCom $=$ hash$(P_d[T + \pi]$.randLocal$)$ for both beacons $d \in \{A, B\}$. If this is false for some Beacon (which is publishable evidence of a Beacon misbehavior), then abort this attempt to combine beacon pulses, else continue.

5. Verify that $P_d[T + \pi]$.previous $= P_d[T]$.randOut for both beacons $d \in \{A, B\}$. If this is false for some Beacon (which is publishable evidence of a Beacon misbehavior), then abort this attempt to combine beacon pulses, else continue.

6. Output the seed Z, defined as:

$$Z \leftarrow \text{hash}(A[T].\text{randOut} \,\|\, B[T].\text{randOut} \,\|\, A[T + \pi].\text{randLocal} \,\|\, B[T + \pi].\text{randLocal} \,\|\, H)$$

When everything goes correctly, the result is a seed that incorporates as pre-image the hash of the committing statement. It also incorporates the randOut fields from $A[T]$ and $B[T]$, which in turn incorporate the sig and ext.value fields from those pulses. The latter two provide authenticity and timeliness guarantees.

Security against one malicious Beacon.   The described procedure enables security even in the face of one malicious beacon (but not both). Suppose beacon A is honest but beacon B is dishonest. Once B has sent $B[T]$, it has committed to at most one value x (satisfying $B[T]$.preCom $=$ hash(x)) to be used in the $B[T + \pi]$.randLocal of the next pulse. This means that if it uses any different value x' in the $B[T + \pi]$.randLocal field of the next pulse the verifications performed by the user will fail in step 4.

Additional considerations.   Additional aspects are deferred to a future separate document. This **MAY** include:

- how to combine many beacons (namely more than two), while being resilient against time-gaps in a few beacons.

- how to combine beacons with different periods and/or with different time offsets (e.g., a beacon that outputs at each 30 seconds mark)?

- possible distinct guidelines for distinct settings, e.g., a user is obtaining randomness for a one-time non-auditable use, vs. a user intends to obtain randomness for future auditability / ability to prove correctness to third parties.

8 Security

2016   In this section we consider the security of the randomness Beacon service. A security
2017   analysis is important to enable reflecting on expressive security claims, helping trust to be
2018   leveled with trustworthiness. Even if beacon operators believe that the system is initialized
2019   in a safe state, we want security to hold in the long run, against conceivable adversarial
2020   threats. For example, some components of the beacon may be compromised as a result
2021   of an external attack, or upon intentional misbehavior of an insider (beacon operator). Some
2022   components of the beacon architecture may also fail spontaneously.

2023   Section 8.1 introduces a characterization of our security model of interest, categorizing
2024   security properties and adversaries. Section 8.2 describes an operational baseline for the
2025   beacon functioning. Attackers may be able to affect the security of the beacon service by
2026   inducing a departure from this baseline. Section 8.3 considers several intrusion scenarios
2027   where essential components of the beacon become compromised. This analysis illustrates
2028   some limits of the beacon security when facing various types of intrusion. Section 8.4
2029   concludes with a few miscellaneous observations.

8.1 Security model

Types of security properties.   Based on the pulse format and beacon interface, we can
conceive an enumeration of desired security properties. We can also consider categories
to which those properties pertain, such as for example:

- **relations** — correct hash chaining and signing, incremental sequencing of indices
  and timestamps, consistent record keeping (authentic past history);

- **availability** — *timely* pulse releases, *accessible* past pulses, *automatic* operations
  (reduced human operator intervention);

- **"rands" quality** — unpredictable, unbiased, fresh and/or independent randomness in
  the randLocal, preCom and randOut fields. (Note: we sometimes use the term *rands*
  as a shortname for the two main random values of interest: randOut and randLocal)

Baseline.   Intuitively, the above mentioned properties follow from the pulse format, in a
baseline uncompromised implementation in which:

- the Beacon App and HSM compute as expected;

- the internal state of the Beacon App and HSM are unbreached;

- the RNGs provide fresh randomness with full entropy;

- the local clock is synchronized with UTC;

- communication is fast and synchronous;

- the databases are available and correct.

2049 **Adversary.** But how to withstand an adversarial compromise of system components? A
2050 security analysis needs to consider cases where subsets of components are compromised, e.g.,
2051 due to adversarial intrusion that makes the system depart from the baseline uncompromised
2052 scenario. It thus matters to characterize the *capabilities* and *goals* of the adversary.

2053 We consider two main types of adversarial behavior upon compromise:

2054 • *semi-honest*, also known as *honest-but-curious* or *passive*, meaning it can exfiltrate
2055   internal state, but without deviating from the protocol specification with respect to
2056   interaction with non-compromised components;

2057 • *malicious*, also known as *active*, meaning that it may have an arbitrary behavior,
2058   including contrary to the beacon specification.

2059 In the remainder, the terms "adversary" and "attacker" are used interchangeably to denote
2060 either a compromised component of the beacon architecture, or an entity that coordinates
2061 information and actions with one or more compromised components. An act of intrusion /
2062 compromise can occur at the onset of a beacon implementation (e.g., by inadvertently using
2063 hardware with an unknown malicious sub-component), or during the beacon operation.

2064 **Adversarial capabilities.** An important characterization of each idealized adversary is
2065 its capability, which includes the control it has over the computational and communication
2066 capabilities of compromised components (e.g., parts of the beacon engine, web frontend,
2067 time server, database, and/or even users) and also the possible access it has to covert
2068 communication channels, computational resources and illegitimately obtained information.

2069 **Adversarial goals.** We focus on five categories of what an attacker "wants":

2070 1. know the future in advance — to predict (or share knowledge of) some randomness
2071   before the time indicated in the timestamp of a pulse;

2072 2. influence the future — to induce with non-negligible probability some property (e.g.,
2073   a bias in 0's) of the random values (`randOut` or `randLocal`) in a pulse;

2074 3. change the past — to alter a previously released pulse without detection, i.e., making
2075   users believe that the pulse in a past time is different from what had already been fixed;

2076 4. fork a chain — to make different users believe in the validity of two different pulses
2077   (e.g., different `randOut`) with same indices (pulse and chain) and timestamp;

2078 5. deny service — to induce the beacon service to become unable to pulsate with the
2079   intended period, possibly even forcing it to end a chain.

2080 This is not an exhaustive list, but it helps us reason about a number of desired operational
2081 defensive-features of the beacon.

2082 **Crypto assumptions.** We also assume the satisfiability of cryptographic assumptions:

2083   • a cryptographic hash is one-way and collision resistant and its output is indistinguish-
2084   able from random when the input is unpredictable;

2085   • the signature scheme is unforgeable and the public-key is unforgeably certified, such
2086   that security against forging signatures depends only on secrecy of the signing key.

2087   8.2   Operational baseline

2088 A number of procedures needed by randomness beacons CAN be modularly conceptualized
2089 in order to describe a reference mode of operation. Some procedures are inherently
2090 related to the rules for generating pulses and the definition of interfaces (as described in
2091 Sections 3 through 6). Other procedures are somewhat independent of the syntax of pulses
2092 and interfaces and apply more generically to operational aspects of putting together all
2093 the components of a beacon implementation. This subsection deals with the latter: key
2094 management, network protocols, time synchronization, and administrative actions (e.g.,
2095 updates, backups and maintenance) and physical configuration.

2096   Each beacon MAY have unique implementation characteristics, regarding the supporting
2097 hardware and software components. This subsection covers high-level operational aspects
2098 that are likely to be applicable to most beacon implementations.

2099   8.2.1   Management of signing keys and certificates

2100 **Key generation and isolation.** Since the authenticity of pulses relies on cryptographic
2101 signatures, it is essential to protect the private signing key in use for each chain. By a
2102 *separation of concerns* principle, the private signing key SHOULD be isolated from the
2103 overall Beacon App. In other words, the ability to sign SHOULD be modularly protected and
2104 separated from the remaining complexity of pulse generation. The Beacon App SHOULD
2105 thus be able to request signatures and obtain a corresponding reply, but SHOULD NOT be
2106 able to to access the actual signing key.

2107 **Certification.** A signing key CAN either be self-signed (self-certified); or certified by an
2108 external certification authority (CA). There MAY exist more than one certificate for each key,
2109 e.g., in order to handle the renovation of certificates across time (ensuring no certification
2110 time-gaps) and/or for applicability to users with different validation requirements. The set
2111 of all certificates for all signing keys ever used to sign pulses must be available to users upon
2112 request — to enable users to validate any past pulse. More concretely, each value ever used
2113 in the `certId` field of a pulse must correspond to a certificate (or vector thereof) that the
2114 beacon service is able to find and provide to a requesting user. Since certificates are public,
2115 they are stored in the publicly accessible Database, and CAN be backed up anywhere else.

2116   The following items are not mandatory for a beacon to operate, but are recommended:

2117   1. **Certification authority (CA).** A Beacon SHOULD obtain from a widely trusted CA a
2118   certificate for its public (signature-verification) key; at least one such public certificate
2119   (but possibly more) SHOULD be valid in any period of pulse generation by a beacon.

2120   2. **Certificate transparency (CT).** The signing-key certificate SHOULD be logged into
2121   a CT [LLK13] log, to promote the detection of conceivable issuance-and-use of rogue
2122   Beacon-signing-key certificates produced by compromised CAs.

2123   3. **Certificate expiration.** It is recommended that any certificate has a validity period
2124   no longer than 5 years from the time of issuance, including because of conceivable
2125   future revisions of approved signature algorithms and parameters.

2126   4. **Certificate revocation.** A Beacon SHOULD publicize its certificate-revocation policy.

2127 **Isolation of the signing capability.**   Given the paramount importance of protecting the
2128 signing key, it is important to ensure its secure isolation and access. This justifies the use of
2129 a signing module, with a controlled interface allowing signature requests by the Beacon App.
2130 This module SHOULD provide a well-defined access-control mechanism, and be capable of
2131 securely performing signatures without key leakage. For example, this MAY be implemented
2132 using a *hardware security module* (HSM) with FIPS 140-2 level 3 certification.

2133   It nonetheless conceivable that a beacon is implemented without the use of a certified
2134 HSM. However, in the remainder we continue referring to an HSM as a possible hardware
2135 device providing intended security properties. Ideally, an HSM would allow generating and
2136 containing the key without it ever leaving the HSM, and possibly even allowing a limitation
2137 of the rate of signatures per amount of time.

2138 ### 8.2.2 Network Security

2139 The flow of information between components of the Beacon requires control. At a first
2140 logical level, some flows are unidirectional, using a push model. For example, the database
2141 receives data sourced at the Beacon App, but not the other way around. There are however
2142 exceptional designated circumstances (e.g., see Section 8.2.4) that warrant a special admin-
2143 istrative mode of operation where, for example, the Beacon App accepts additional input,
2144 e.g., for reposition of accidentally lost state.

2145   The network connections SHOULD, as much as possible, be dedicated and isolated from
2146 unrelated services. This can be particularly helpful in reducing the surface for potential attack
2147 initiated from other components. It can also help with reducing the delay of communications.

2148 ### 8.2.3 Time synchronization

2149 A secure beacon service offers two main features related to time: it generates pulses as late
2150 as possible to enable a timely release; it releases pulses not before the time indicated in the
2151 timeStamp field. These features require the ability to reliably measure time. At a logical
2152 level, this can be comprised to an assumption that the local clock of the beacon engine has
2153 (relative to an intended precision) a small enough offset from UTC. At a practical level, the
2154 implementation must explicitly provision for a correct synchronization of the local clock.

2155   We enumerate here three vectors for accomplishing synchronization:

1. use the network time protocol (NTP) to interactively synchronize with a time server assumed to have the correct UTC time;

2. use a non-interactive protocol, using the time read from a receive-only signal, such as based on the global positioning system (GPS);

3. use a local clock certified to have time drift less than a certain threshold, throughout a long duration;

These three options are not mutually exclusive, and CAN conceivably be combined. Correspondingly, some adversarial capabilities may enable time manipulation attacks [MCBG16].

8.2.4 Maintenance, availability and recoverability

Updates and downtime. The software and hardware platform of an implemented Beacon service MAY require updates (e.g., security patches, replacement) at diverse moments in time. Such actions CAN induce downtime of the beacon service, e.g., if an update requires a reboot of the operating system that underlies the Beacon App. For example:

- **Power outages in beacon engine.** If the Beacon Engine temporarily losses of power, then then the pulse generation will be stopped temporarily. Skipping the generation of pulses for some time leads to time *gaps* in an active chain.

- **Externally-inaccessible database.** If the external database is temporarily unavailable frmo the outside, then users will not have access to the beacon pulses during some time. In the latter case the generation of pulses CAN still remain without gaps, and at a later stage the produced pulses become available for consultation.

Since availability is itself a security aspect, the above considerations justify a balance between frequency of updates and the resulting frequency of gaps.

Backups and recoverability. It is crucial to ensure the long-term availability of public records of the beacon, including pulses and associated data. Thus, an essential aspect of availability pertains to actual loss of information, e.g., a database loss due to problems with the underlying storage medium. Since the records have an "unlimited" lifetime, there must exist backups of the database(s). Two distinct possibilities are enumerated here:

- to enhance continuous (and real-time) availability, a state-machine replication implementation CAN enable data access even when one database replica (out of several) fails;

- to enhance long-term availability, regardless of possible temporary downtimes, a state recovery protocol CAN define how to replace a failed component, and how to setup its initial state to match that of an offline or online backup replica.

A special case pertains to the Beacon App memory, which in normal functioning SHOULD not receive information (about pulses) from outside of the Beacon Engine. Some of the records therein, pertaining to some past pulses (previous, hour, day, month, year),

2193 are needed for the generation of new pulses. If this memory is lost, e.g., if the memory
2194 modules irrecoverably fail, then a replacement will have to be updated with an initial state
2195 (unless a new chain starts). Such setup is an example of an administrative action with a flow
2196 of information contrary to the one mentioned in Section 8.2.2.

2197   With respect to the internal storage of the beacon app, it is worth noticing a difference
2198 between the loss of randLocal and the loss of past output values. Since randLocal is
2199 (by design) not present in previous pulses, it CANNOT be recovered from them. For this
2200 reason, there is an exception provisioned for the case of loss of randLocal: the next pulse
2201 proceeds by filling the first bit-flag of status with value 1, meaning "randLocal without
2202 corresponding preCom", and omitting the randLocal value (i.e., filling it with all zeros).
2203 Except for the first pulse in a chain, we do not allow not including past output values.

2204   8.2.5   Boundaries and Physical Security

2205 **Recommendation (access boundaries).** The access boundaries of the system SHOULD
2206 be well defined, to help enumerating conceivable attack vectors that may exploit
2207 permeabilities thereof. A relevant defense line pertains to physical security measures,
2208 limiting the possible physical attacks and deterring certain types of insider attacks. It is thus
2209 encouraged that each administrative domain of a beacon defines a physical security policy
2210 for its beacon implementation. This MAY include defining rules of access to the beacon
2211 machinery, and corresponding audit rules (e.g., based on access logs). For example, should
2212 there be a guard determining who can enter the room and logging all entries? How should
2213 the access logs be audited, and by whom?

2214 **Recommendation (ability to shutdown).** A Beacon SHOULD be setup with the ability
2215 for human beacon operators to physically shutdown the service, and to be able to signal to
2216 the outside world that such shutdown will, is or has occur(ed) (somewhat equivalent to a
2217 key revocation operation). Conversely, it is possible to conceive a fully virtualized beacon
2218 implementation, following the reference format and running in completely autonomous
2219 mode, without human operators being able to shut it down after bootstrap.

2220   8.3   Intrusion scenarios

2221 We now consider intrusion scenarios where a subset of components becomes compromised:

2222   1. Malicious Beacon App → full-bias attack on randLocal

2223   2. Malicious Beacon App → full prediction and exfiltration attack

2224   3. Malicious Beacon App → bias attack on randOut

2225   4. Malicious time along with compromised database → "rands" prediction attack

2226   5. Semi-honest Beacon App → "rands" prediction attack

2227   6. Malicious database knowing the signing key → change-history attack

2228 **8.3.1   Malicious Beacon App → full bias on randLocal**

2229 **Specification.**   The value $r_{i+1} = P_{i+1}.\text{randLocal}$ released in pulse P_{i+1} is the hash pre-
2230 image of the value $C_i = P_i.\text{preCom}$ released in pulse P_i. Supposedly, this randLocal value
2231 r_{i+1} is computed as $\rho_i' \equiv \text{Hash}(\rho_{1,i} \,||\, \rho_{2,i} \,[||\, \rho_{3,i}])$, where the (at least two) values $\rho_{j,i}$ are the
2232 "raw" outputs from the several RNGs learned by the Beacon App (but not revealed outside)
2233 during the process of generating pulse P_i.

2234 **Attack vector.**   Since the "raws" are not revealed outside, a malicious Beacon App can
2235 undetectably ignore them and decide an arbitrary randLocal ρ_i and then hash it to obtain
2236 C_i. The compromise scenario is depicted in Fig. 9.

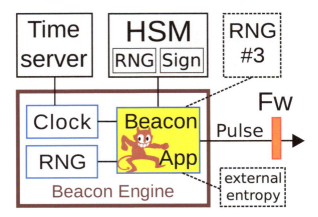

Figure 9. Illustration of malicious Beacon App

2237 **Mitigation in place.**   The rules for combining beacons (Section 7.4) specify that
2238 randLocal **SHOULD** only be used to combine randomness from different beacons. The
2239 result of the combination leads to good randomness if at least one beacon is uncompromised.
2240 Nonetheless, the fact the randLocal can be fully biased by a malicious beacon **SHOULD**
2241 be an explicit consideration by users. This is specially relevant in the face of adversaries
2242 capable of affecting several beacons.

2243   The trustworthiness on a beacon providing unbiasable randomness **SHOULD** be distinct
2244 when comparing randLocal vs. randOut. A malicious Beacon App can fully determine
2245 the value randLocal, while it only has limited bias on randOut (see Section 8.3.3). In
2246 particular, such compromise **CAN** lead the beacon to become deterministic (if using a
2247 deterministic signature algorithm), during the periods without change of external.value
2248 and certificateId.

2249 **A conceivable mitigation requiring changing the calculation of a field value.**   The men-
2250 tioned attack would be prevented with a conceivable simple redefinition of the calculation
2251 of randLocal (without additional fields). This, however, requires a change in the format
2252 specification and is thus conceived only for a potential future version of the format.

2253   The idea is to make $randLocal_{i+1}$ not be simply the pre-image of $preCom_i$ but rather the
2254 XOR of the pre-image and $randOut_i$. Then, even a malicious Beacon App could not fully
2255 control the value $randLocal$, while still committing to it in a verifiable manner. Concretely,
2256 we would have the following:

2257   • (as currently done) $\rho_i = \text{hash}(\rho_{i,1} || \rho_{i,2} [|| \rho_{i,3}...])$

2258   • (as currently done) $P_i.\text{preCom} = \text{hash}(\rho_i)$

2259   • (as a change) $P_{i+1}.randLocal = \rho_i \oplus P_i.randOut$ (instead of $P_{i+1}.randLocal = \rho_i$)

2260   This means that when a malicious Beacon App chooses the value $randLocal$ it still
2261 does not know the resulting value P_{i+1}, which will then be obtained upon a hash calcula-
2262 tion. Since $\oplus$ is a computationally-invertible permutation, the verification by users is still
2263 straightforward, by simply defining $\rho_i = P_i.randOut \oplus P_{i+1}.randLocal$ and then checking
2264 that $\text{hash}(\rho_i) = P_i.\text{preCom}$.

2265   As a further benefit, in this scenario the value of $randLocal$ depends on the use of the
2266 HSM, which allows limiting further the possible bias that a malicious Beacon App can
2267 induce, as already described in Section 8.3.3 for $randOut$. This mitigation thus equalizes the
2268 amount of bias that the Beacon has with respect to the two rands ($randOut$ and $randLocal$).

2269 8.3.2 Malicious Beacon App → full prediction and exfiltration attack

2270 As mentioned in Section 8.3.1, a malicious Beacon App can undetectably decide in advance
2271 the value $randLocal$ of each pulse, provided it presents a corresponding $preCom$ in the
2272 previous pulse.

2273   In fact, a malicious Beacon App can for example define $randLocal$ as an enciphering
2274 of a counter, e.g., $\rho_i = \text{Enc}_K(i)$, where Enc is a block-cipher with appropriate output length,
2275 K is a secret key shared with an outside adversary, and i is the counter. The adversary
2276 can then predict in advance all values $P_i.randLocal$ for any i. This also means there is no
2277 assurance on $randOut$ being fresh, unbiased or unpredictable.

2278   This attack vector also allows the beacon App to exfiltrate internal state that it may learn
2279 about the Beacon Engine. Particularly, it can use it to covertly communicate with an outside
2280 party, encrypting information into a ciphertext that is indistinguishable from random and
2281 which can only be read by the outsider.

2282   It is worth noticing that the mitigation technique (different calculation of $randLocal$)
2283 presented in Section 8.3.1, while capable of preventing the full bias of $randLocal$ is not
2284 sufficient to prevent the exfiltration or full prediction attack.

2285 8.3.3 Malicious Beacon App → bias on $randOut$

2286 **Attack vector.** A malicious Beacon App, with access to a honest HSM, can generate many
2287 pulses in advance, by simply not waiting enough between each signing request. The Beacon
2288 App can thus try many different values of $randLocal$ and produce different signature

2289   requests to the HSM, until obtaining a signature whose respective hash — the randOut
2290   value — will have a particular property. For example, if the HSM has the capability (e.g., as
2291   a feature of rapid cryptographic operations) to perform about 2^{20} signatures per minute, then
2292   the malicious Beacon App can induce the result of the final randOut to satisfy a predicate
2293   that happens about once in a million in average (e.g., all zeros in the twenty least significant
2294   bits). Since the Beacon App can also accelerate the generation of pulses, it can conceivably
2295   first compute a full day worth of pulses and then perform the bias attack on the pulse for the
2296   next day, therefore gaining control over about 10 more bits.

2297   **Mitigations.**   One possible mitigation is to have an HSM (or even simply a proxy) that
2298   induces a mandatory delay between signing requests, and/or which limits the number of
2299   allowed signing requests per established session.

2300   Another conceivable mitigation is to partition the Beacon App in a way that a component
2301   that requests the signature never gets to see the signature result. If the beacon operator has
2302   control over the network communication flow, then it may prevent a malicious intruder from
2303   communicating across those two components, therefore effectively preventing the signature-
2304   requester component from knowing whether or not it should request a new signature.

2305   ### 8.3.4   Malicious time along with compromised database $\rightarrow$ rands prediction

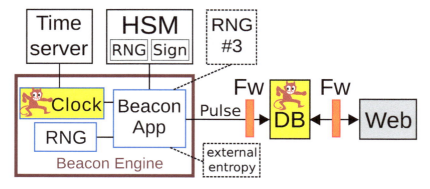

Figure 10. Illustration of malicious clock and database

2306   **Attack vector (malicious local-clock).**   We describe an attack where the Beacon App and
2307   HSM remain honest, but the local clock and the (internal or external) database become
2308   compromised. The compromise scenario is depicted in Fig. 10.

2309   A malicious local clock can for example induce the generation of an entire-day pulse-set
2310   in a single hour. For each generated pulse, the honest Beacon App then releases the pulses
2311   to the internal database, unaware that they were released ahead of time. After enough
2312   generated pulses in advance, the malicious clock can slow down until becoming again
2313   synchronized with UTC.

2314   A semi-honest database can leak the anticipated knowledge to an adversary, thus
2315 breaking the unpredictability property. A malicious database and-or web interface can
2316 also delay the release of the anticipated pulses to users, thereby making the compromise
2317 undetectable. The beacon operators and users never detect that a time-skew occurred and
2318 that pulses were generated in advance.

2319 **Possible mitigations.**

2320 • **Authenticated clock.** By having the Beacon App use an external authenticated clock,
2321   the forward time skew would not possible. The Beacon App would only accept
2322   timestamps already validated by some trusted signature.

2323 • **Authenticated timestamps, via** `ext.value`. Another mitigation is to periodically
2324   incorporate authenticated timestamps into the pulse, via the `ext.value` field mech-
2325   anism. Concretely, one CAN define an external source (`ext.srcId`) that describes
2326   using an authenticated timestamp as the hash pre-image of `ext.value`, at particular
2327   moments in time. This would allows external users to verify that the pulses were only
2328   generated after the Beacon App had knowledge of the authenticated timestamp. Con-
2329   ceivably, this CAN also be done based on randomness values from different beacons,
2330   which by the specification in this document are authenticated by the respective beacons.
2331   The use of an authenticated/timestamps output value from at least one uncompromised
2332   beacon would be sufficient to guarantee unanticipated pulse generation.

2333 **Another attack vector (honest local-clock, malicious time-server).** Even with an intact
2334 beacon engine, a timing attack can be launched from a malicious external time-server, outside
2335 of the beacon engine. Suppose that the Beacon App relies on its underlying operating system
2336 (OS) to control "sleep" system calls, trusting that the OS will "awake" the App at the
2337 intended time. Suppose also that the OS, in control of the local clock, is responsible for
2338 initiating the time-synch protocol with the time-server. The time server can then induce an
2339 undetectable skew rate, which will depend on the time-synch scheduling frequency.

2340   For simplicity we assume the case of a 1 minute period between pulses. For an un-
2341 detectable attack, each synchronization cannot skew the time forward by more than one
2342 minute, or otherwise it would induce a time gap in the chain, which would be detectable.
2343 For example, suppose the OS only requests synchronization approximately once every two
2344 minutes. The local-clock time is then limited to advance, in average, at 1.5 times the speed
2345 of regular time. This means that for a single hour the clock is not able to skew more than
2346 30 minutes, i.e., about 30 pulses. If instead the synchronization happens once every 10
2347 seconds, then the rate can be has high as about 6 times. The consequences are more restricted
2348 than the case of the attack described with a fully malicious clock. Some consequences /
2349 detectability of the attack may be implementation-specific, e.g., depending on whether the
2350 sleep/awake actions depend on timestamps vs. computation cycles. If the communication
2351 in the time-synchronization protocol is not protected, then it is enough to have a malicious
2352 intrusion of the network channel.

Mitigation.   The attack described in the case of a malicious local clock included a second phase where the clock would slowly get back into the correct time. A Beacon App CAN conceivably be programmed to analyze clock adjustments and throw an exception when detecting too many (too large) time-skews, backward and forward. For example, a Beacon App CAN be defined to alert the Beacon operator if detecting that in a 2 minute span (according to local-clock time) the time-synch operation lead to a time-skew greater than 10 seconds. This would further reduce the possible skew rate of anticipated production/release of pulses.

8.3.5   Semi-honest Beacon App → rands prediction

Advanced knowledge of rands.   Within the operational guidelines for timely generation and release of pulses (see Fig. 3 in Section 3.3), it is unavoidable that a semi-honest Beacon App has privileged knowledge of randLocal during a time window up to $\pi + \Delta$ (i.e., in advance of allowed time for pulse release); it also has privileged knowledge of randOut for a time window of up to $\max(0, \Delta - \gamma)$.

Some mitigations — possible and conceivable.

- **M1 (possible).   Adequate parametrization of generation and release time.** As already recommended in Section A.1, the generation and release parameters SHOULD be adjusted to allow smaller windows of predictability. Making $\gamma > \Delta$ removes the predictability of randOut by a semi-honest Beacon App. (Compare Fig. 11 vs. Fig. 3.) However, this does not eliminate the predictability of randLocal. Even in the extreme of choosing $\Delta \leq 0$ (not depicted in Fig. 11), i.e., starting the generation only after the allowed release time, $randLocal_{i+1}$ would still be learned before the whole pulse P_i.

- **M2 (conceivable): A slight change in randLocal definition.** Section 8.3.1 suggested a simple change in the calculation of $randLocal_{i+1}$, where it becomes equal to the XOR of $randOut_i$ and the pre-image of $preCom_i$. Then, the value of randLocal would only be learned after the pulse is generated. This reduces slightly the time-window of advanced knowledge (See "case M2" in Fig. 11)

- **M3 (conceivable future).   A radical change in randLocal definition.** The predictability of randLocal against a semi-honest Beacon App could be eliminated upon a significant change in the definition of randLocal, and depending on further capabilities by the HSM. The idea is to let $randLocal_{i+1}$ be defined as a pre-image of a one-way permutation with trapdoor that requires the help of the HSM only after a pulse has been computed, and such that the value is nonetheless still committed by $preCom_i$. Let (K_{sec}, K_{pub}) be a new secret/public key pair for a one-way trapdoor permutation $\mathscr{P}$; let K_{sec} be protected by the HSM, never revealed to the Beacon App, but usable by the HSM upon request the Beacon App. The new randLocal is computed by the Beacon App as follows:

    - as usual, obtain $r_{i+1} = \mathrm{hash}(\rho_{i,1} || \rho_{i,2} [|| \rho_{i,3} ...])$;
    - as usual, publish $preCom_i = \mathrm{hash}(r_{i+1})$ in pulse P_i;

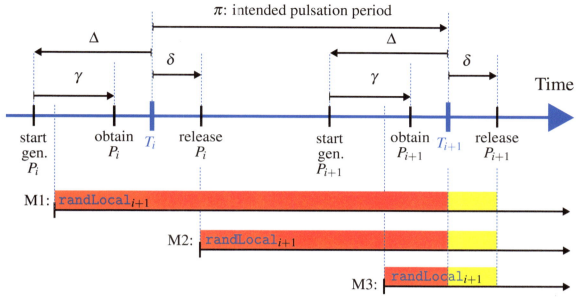

Legend: red rectangles (window of predictability of `randLocal`); Let $r_{i+1} = \mathrm{hash}(\rho_{i,1}||\rho_{i,2}[||\rho_{i,3}...])$ and `preCom`$_i$ = $\mathrm{hash}(r_{i+1})$. Then, `randLocal`$_{i+1}$ equals: r_{i+1} in M1; $r_{i+1} \oplus$ `randOut`$_i$ in M2; $\mathscr{P}_{K_{sec}}^{-1}(r_{i+1})$ in M3.

Figure 11. Different predictabilities for different `randLocal` formulas

– as part of computing P_{i+1}, and by using $\gamma \approx \Delta$, wait till very close to `timeStamp`$_{i+1}$ to query the HSM for `randLocal`$_{i+1} = \mathscr{P}_{K_{sec}}^{-1}(r_{i+1})$.

– continue the computation of P_{i+1} and release it shortly after time `timeStamp`$_{i+1}$

The verifiability equation for users is then $\mathrm{hash}(\mathscr{P}_{K_{pub}}(\mathrm{randLocal}_{i+1})) \overset{?}{=} \mathrm{preCom}_i$, because $r_{i+1} = \mathscr{P}_{K_{pub}}(\mathscr{P}_{K_{sec}}^{-1}(r_{i+1}))$. Since a semi-honest Beacon App queries the HSM only after `timeStamp`$_{i+1}$, it only learns `randLocal`$_{i+1}$ at that time, therefore reducing the predictability time-window. By using appropriate timing parameters, this could effectively reduce to 0 the window of predictability, with respect to the allowed release time `timeStamp`+$_{i+1}$.

8.3.6 Malicious database and leaked signing key → change-history attack

A conceivable stealing of the HSM key. Suppose an insider attacker has temporary physical access (e.g., less than a minute) to the HSM and to the administrator and operator cards of the HSM, along with corresponding pass-phrases. By connecting to the HSM using the stolen credentials, the attacker can backup the module key. Suppose the attacker also gains access to the key-blob (which is also backed up, in encrypted format, possibly in the cloud). The attacker can now hide, decrypt the key-blob offline and produce signatures on its own.

A complementary attack vector is conceivable depending on the policy for renewing/backing up/copying the module key. If there is a secondary HSM with the same module key, there is a larger attack surface to steal/replicate the module key.

2411   The compromise scenario is depicted in Fig. 12.

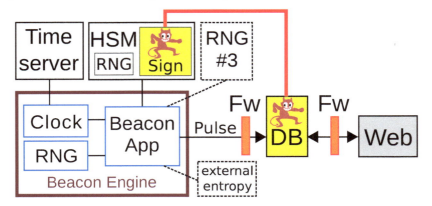

Figure 12. Illustration of malicious database and leaked signing key

2412 **A conceivable change-history attack.**   Suppose the attacker is further able to maliciously
2413 compromise the internal or external database (already away from the beacon engine). If the
2414 attacker knows the HSM signing key, it is then able to choose any past or present point in the
2415 chain (pulse i) and replace the whole chain from that point onward. The new chain satisfies all
2416 needed relational properties. The different chain produced by the Beacon App never gets out.

2417   The attack can then completely ignore future pulses produced by the Beacon App. This
2418 succeeds because the Beacon App does not receive feedback from the outside.

2419 **A possible mitigation.**   If the attacker changes past pulses that have already been sent
2420 outside, then it is at risk of a user finding a non-repudiable inconsistency. However, there is
2421 no guarantee that a single user tricked by the a ttacker is able to confirm what other users
2422 have already received. A mitigation to this is to improve the ability for users to obtain pulses
2423 stored by external repositories. For example, if the first pulse of each day is stored in some
2424 high-reliable public website, then it CAN serve as anchor to verify any past pulse. A beacon
2425 CAN provide information about these anchors in order to have the user verify a skiplist
2426 connecting the anchor to the target past value.

2427 **8.4 Other recommendations**

2428   • **Not a random oracle.** A theoretical public random oracle (in the usual sense) would
2429   not know the hash pre-image of the outputted randomness. However, in the case of
2430   the Beacon here defined the actual pre-image is part of the procedure of verifying
2431   correctness. This means that the randomness CAN be used in applications where the
2432   knowledge of the hash pre-image is not a problem.

2433   • **Code review.** Since the Beacon is a public service, it is recommended that the
2434   software code of the Beacon App be published (e.g., open source) for external review
2435   by the community. This CAN be done without prejudice of retaining privacy of certain
2436   security parameterizations, such as firewall configurations, time-synch schedules, etc.

2437 ## 9 Future considerations

2438 In settling a concrete version 2.0.0, some design decisions were taken on the side of
2439 restricting functionality. This section describes a few identified items whose consideration
2440 may benefit from feedback from stake-holders, and may motivate changes in future versions.

2441 1. **Cipher suite values.**   Allow new values for the `cipher` field.   Any update
2442 **SHOULD** reflect an update of the sub-version (value z in the version number 2.y.z),
2443 while y **NEED NOT** change. Existing chains continue as is, since the `cipher` value
2444 **SHALL NOT** change within a chain. Conceivable updates include allowing ECC-based
2445 signatures, post-quantum safe signatures, threshold signatures and SHA3 hashes.
2446 Advantages include reducing the size and increasing the security; disadvantages
2447 include increased complexity for supporting the full suite of allowed algorithms.

2448 2. **Hash values zero.** For conciseness, allow a hash zero to be serialized as a simple
2449 (uint64) encoding of length C, i.e., indicating that no hash follows. In the current
2450 specification, whenever a hashOut field is not applicable (e.g., sometimes for
2451 `ext.srcId`, `ext.value`, `randLocal`, ...) it is instead being filled with an all-zeros
2452 string (i.e., exactly *BLenHash* bytes with value zero).

2453 3. **Other past output values.** Enable a dynamic specification of which past output
2454 values are included in the pre-image of the `randOut`. For example, if a chain outputs
2455 pulses with a period of five seconds (12 times faster than the current NIST beacon),
2456 then it may be useful to also include as past value the first pulse with the same time-
2457 with-minute-precision as the previous pulse. Conversely, a chain that outputs one pulse
2458 per hour could dispense the `out.H` field; a chain that outputs one pulse per day could
2459 also dispense the `out.D` field. This can be achieved with a change in format that would
2460 enable parsing the number of past output values that follow, and identifying the time re-
2461 lation with the previous pulse (and/or the pulse index difference with the current pulse).

2462 4. **Multiple certificates.**   Explain how the reply to a query for the certificate(s)
2463 corresponding to a `certificateId` value **CAN** include multiple certificates. In the
2464 current document, the description of the PEM file (the hash pre-image of `certId`)
2465 assumes a single certificate for the signature key. Advantages in allowing several
2466 simultaneous certificates to be valid (and verifiable), for the same key in use, include:

2467 (a) It widens the scope of acceptability of pulses, since it allows validation of
2468 pulses by different external users that have different requirements on certificate
2469 acceptance. This is likely to happen when different external users are from
2470 administratively independent jurisdictions, e.g., different countries, with
2471 stringent legal requirements (e.g., what can be accepted in a court of law).

2472 (b) It allows for simultaneous use of different certification technologies, e.g.,
2473 conceivable future use of some experimental post-quantum secure certificate,
2474 along side with continuing to use a standard certification technology.

2475 (c) It allows use of several keys in some kind of multi/threshold signatures where
2476 it may be useful to account for several public keys.

71

References

[BCG15] J. Bonneau, J. Clark, and S. Goldfeder. *On Bitcoin as a public randomness source.* Cryptology ePrint Archive, Report 2015/1015, 2015. https://eprint.iacr.org/2015/1015.

[BDF+15] T. Baignères, C. Delerablée, M. Finiasz, L. Goubin, T. Lepoint, and M. Rivain. *Trap Me If You Can – Million Dollar Curve.* Cryptology ePrint Archive, Report 2015/1249, 2015. https://eprint.iacr.org/2015/1249.

[BLFM05] T. Berners-Lee, R. Fielding, and L. Masinter. *Uniform Resource Identifier (URI): Generic Syntax.* RFC 3986, January 2005. DOI:10.17487/RFC3986.

[Blu81] M. Blum. *Coin flipping by telephone.* A Report on CRYPTO 81, pages 11–15, 1981. Also at COMPCON'82, pp. 133-137, IEEE, 1982. Also as "Coin flipping by telephone – a protocol for solving impossible problems." at SIGACT News, 15:23–27, 1983, DOI:10.1145/1008908.1008911.

[BNM+14] J. Bonneau, A. Narayanan, A. Miller, J. Clark, J. A. Kroll, and E. W. Felten. *Mixcoin: Anonymity for Bitcoin with accountable mixes.* In International Conference on Financial Cryptography and Data Security, pages 486–504. Springer, 2014.

[CD17] I. Cascudo and B. David. *SCRAPE: Scalable Randomness Attested by Public Entities.* In D. Gollmann, A. Miyaji, and H. Kikuchi (eds.), Applied Cryptography and Network Security – ACNS, pages 537–556. Springer International Publishing, 2017. DOI:10.1007/978-3-319-61204-1˙27.

[CH10] J. Clark and U. Hengartner. *On the Use of Financial Data As a Random Beacon.* In Proceedings of the 2010 International Conference on Electronic Voting Technology/Workshop on Trustworthy Elections, EVT/WOTE'10, pages 1–8, Berkeley, CA, USA, 2010. USENIX Association.

[CLC18] CLCERT. *CLCERT Randomness Beacon Project*, 2018.

[CSF+08] D. Cooper, S. Santesson, S. Farrell, S. Boeyen, R. Housley, and W. Polk. *Internet X.509 Public Key Infrastructure Certificate and CRL Profile.* RFC, 5280(5280):1–151, May 2008. DOI:10.17487/RFC5280.

[Haa18] M. Haahr. *RANDOM.ORG: True Random Number Service*, 1998–2018.

[HL93] A. Herzberg and M. Luby. *Public Randomness in Cryptography.* In E. F. Brickell (ed.), Advances in Cryptology — CRYPTO' 92, vol. 740 of LNCS, pages 421–432. Springer Berlin Heidelberg, 1993. DOI:10.1007/3-540-48071-4˙29.

[INM18] INMETRO. *Brazilian Randomness Beacon Project (FAPESP)*, 2018.

[KTY04] A. Kiayias, Y. Tsiounis, and M. Yung. *Traceable Signatures.* In C. Cachin and J. L. Camenisch (eds.), Advances in Cryptology - EUROCRYPT 2004, pages 571–589, Berlin, Heidelberg, 2004. Springer Berlin Heidelberg. DOI:10.1007/978-3-540-24676-3˙34.

[LLK13] B. Laurie, A. Langley, and E. Kasper. *Certificate Transparency.* RFC, 6962(6962), June 2013. DOI:10.17487/RFC6962.

[MCBG16] A. Malhotra, I. E. Cohen, E. Brakke, and S. Goldberg. *Attacking the Network Time Protocol.* In NDSS, 2016.

[MN10] T. Moran and M. Naor. *Split-ballot Voting: Everlasting Privacy with Distributed Trust.* ACM Trans. Inf. Syst. Secur., 13(2):16:1–16:43, March 2010. DOI:10.1145/1698750.1698756. See prior version at CCS'07, DOI:10.1145/1315245.1315277.

[NIS13a] NIST. *FIPS 186-4, Digital Signature Standard (DSS), Federal Information Processing Standard (FIPS) Publication.* Technical report, Department of Commerce, 2013. DOI:10.6028/NIST.FIPS.186-4.

[NIS13b] NIST. *FIPS 186-5, Digital Signature Standard (DSS), Federal Information Processing Standard (FIPS) Publication.* Technical report, Department of Commerce, 2013. DOI:10.6028/NIST.FIPS.186-4. (Expected to appear in May 2019).

[NIS15] NIST. *FIPS 180-4, Secure Hash Standard, Federal Information Processing Standard (FIPS) Publication.* Technical report, Department of Commerce, 2015. DOI:10.6028/NIST.FIPS.180-4.

[NIS18] NIST. *NIST Randomness Beacon Project*, 2013–2018.

[NK02] C. Newman and G. Klyne. *Date and Time on the Internet: Timestamps.* RFC 3339, July 2002. DOI:10.17487/RFC3339.

[Rab83] M. O. Rabin. *Transaction protection by beacons.* Journal of Computer and System Sciences, 27(2):256–267, 1983. DOI:10.1016/0022-0000(83)90042-9.

[SJK+17] E. Syta, P. Jovanovic, E. K. Kogias, N. Gailly, L. Gasser, I. Khoffi, M. J. Fischer, and B. Ford. *Scalable bias-resistant distributed randomness.* In IEEE (ed.), Security and Privacy (SP), 2017 IEEE Symposium on, pages 444–460, 2017. DOI:10.1109/SP.2017.45.

[SJSW18] P. Schindler, A. Judmayer, N. Stifter, and E. Weippl. *HydRand: Practical Continuous Distributed Randomness.* Cryptology ePrint Archive, Report 2018/319, 2018. https://eprint.iacr.org/2018/319.

[Yer03] F. Yergeau. *UTF-8, a transformation format of ISO 10646.* RFC 3629, STD 63, November 2003. DOI:10.17487/RFC3629.

Appendix A   Implementation recommendations

A.1   Recommendations about generation and release timeline

The promises in Section 3.3 leave some implementation flexibility. For example: in an extreme with $(\Delta, \delta) = (\pi, \pi/4)$, a slow pulse generation could use time equal to up to five fourths of a period (i.e., $\gamma \leq 5\pi/4$); in the opposite extreme, an ideal generation/release timeline would, if assuming no skew to UTC, have $(\Delta, \delta, \gamma) \approx (0, 0, 0)$, with $\delta \geq 0$.

In contrast to the allowed flexibility, it is useful that a Beacon has a predictable rate and that it releases pulses as close as possible to the indicated timestamp, provided it satisfies the promises. Therefore, in the following we put forward several recommendations to promote more concrete expectations and interoperable implementations.

The following *recommendations* represent *aspirational implementation goals*, rather than promises. The goals MAY possibly be overruled by other implementation concerns specific to each Beacon implementation. For example, some time uncertainty about asynchronous communications in the beacon engine MAY lead a beacon operator to set additional safety margin with respect to generation or release time (while compliant with the promises).

Need to handle the clock skew.   A detailed analysis SHOULD consider the maximum estimated skew (σ), of the local clock, with respect to UTC. The actual skew will depend on the quality of the local clock, on the synchronization frequency, and on the synchronization protocol. For the most part, we simply assume that the time-server used as reference for UTC synchronization is itself accurately synchronized with UTC, but in Section 8.3.4 we consider the case of malicious compromise of the time server.

Hard time-recommendations.   Let σ^+ and σ^- respectively represent reasonable majorants for the maximum absolute skew ahead (σ^+) and behind (σ^-) of UTC. Then, take the necessary precautions to ensure:

- **R1 — Avoid too-large skew:** $\sigma^+ < \pi/10$ and $\sigma^- < \pi/10$.
- **R2 — Avoid too-early release** ($\approx$ **Promise 1**): $\delta \geq \sigma^-$
- **R3 — Avoid too-late release** ($\approx$ **Promise 3**): $\max(\delta, \gamma - \Delta) < \pi/4 - \sigma^+$
- **R4 — Avoid too-early generation start** ($\approx$ **Promise 4**): $\Delta < \pi - \sigma^+-$

Soft time-recommendations (fine-tuning).   Conditioned to the hard time-recommendations, try to fine-tune the implementation to enable timing parameters to minimize η and η', subject to the following conditions:

- **R5 — Minimize the skew:** $0 \leq \sigma^-, \sigma^+ \leq \eta$
- **R6 — Minimize the release instant:** $0 \leq \delta - \sigma^- \leq \eta$
- **R7 — Maximize the generation start instant:** $0 \leq \Delta - \gamma - \sigma^+ \leq \eta$

2579   • **R8 — Minimize the generation duration:** $0 \leq \gamma \leq \eta'$

2580   Recall that in R8 the parameter γ denotes the time taken between initiating the sampling
2581 of randomness from the local RNGs and obtaining the full pulse (including the signature
2582 and respective hash).

2583 **Definition (tuning slack)**   A Beacon engine satisfying recommendations (R5, R6 and
2584 R7) for some parameter value η is said to be within *tuning slack η*. Except when noticed
2585 otherwise, η is expressed in seconds.

2586   Note that recommendations R5, R6 and R7 are about deciding when to do something,
2587 whereas recommendation R8 is about the time that a computation takes.

2588 **Definition (time accuracy)**   A Beacon Engine is said to have *time accuracy* within α if
2589 $\alpha \geq \max(\Delta - \gamma - \sigma^-, \delta' + \sigma^+)$, where $\delta' = \max(\delta, \gamma - \Delta)$. In other words, *time accuracy*
2590 within α means that the generation-time start time and the maximum release time are both
2591 (relative to the assumed duration γ and to the `timeStamp` value of the corresponding pulse)
2592 distanced to the optimal values by a value that is bounded by α. Except when noticed
2593 otherwise, α is expressed in seconds.

2594   Note: the auxiliary definition for δ' is just to account for a possible misconfiguration of
2595 other parameters; in practice, it does not make sense to define (δ, γ, Δ) such that $\gamma - \Delta > \delta$;
2596 in regular parameterizations one will always have $\delta = \delta'$.

2597 **Examples of acceptable and non-acceptable parametrizations.**   As a way of example
2598 for beacon operators, Table 13 exemplifies several conceivable timing parameterizations that
2599 are acceptable within the scope of promises and hard recommendations. Correspondingly,
2600 Table 14 shows unacceptable parameterizations, when some hard recommendation fails.
2601 The values are merely illustrative. In practice it is always desirable to ensure that the skew
2602 is lower than 1 second.

2603 **Generation-start not after** `timeStamp`.   Row #4 is an example where there is an
2604 inactivity gap between the end of the generation (at $t = 2$) and the release (at $t = 3$), since
2605 $\delta > \gamma - \Delta$. It would be conceivable to decide $\Delta = -1$ (i.e, to have a negative value) to
2606 remove the gap, without delaying the release. However, while ensuring that the important
2607 promise of no early release is met, we decide for having a gap as a way to ensure that a
2608 correct clock (i.e., without skew during this generation, regardless of σ^- and σ^+) starts
2609 the generation process not after `timeStamp`.

2610 **Other factors to consider.**   A decision of timing parameters CAN depend on other factors,
2611 such as the possible variability in the duration of pulse generation (γ), and/or the accuracy
2612 of "awake" times ($T - \Delta$ and $T + \delta$) upon a "sleep" system call. Other timing adjustments
2613 MAY also happen after a time synchronization, and/or due to asynchronous interactions.

Table 13. Examples of acceptable timing parametrizations

#	π	Δ	γ	δ	σ^-	σ^+	Recomm. R1 R2 R3 R4	Conceivable intervals Generation	Release	Slack (η)	Accuracy (α)
1	60	0.2	0.1	0.1	0.1	0.1	Y Y Y Y	$[-0.3,0]$	$[0,0.2]$	0.1	0.2
2	60	2	1	1	1	1	Y Y Y Y	$[-3,0]$	$[0,2]$	1	2
3	60	0	1	1	1	1	Y Y Y Y	$[-1,2]$	$[0,2]$	1	2
4	60	1	2	1	1	1	Y Y Y Y	$[-2,2]$	$[0,2]$	1	2
5	60	5	2	3	3	1	Y Y Y Y	$[-8,2]$	$[0,4]$	3	4
6	60	30	15	8	2	2	Y Y Y Y	$[-32,-13]$	$[6,10]$	28	13
7	60	59	5	0.5	0.5	0.5	Y Y Y Y	$[-59.5,-53.5]$	$[0,1]$	58.5	53.5

Legend: All values are in seconds; N (No); Y (Yes). The conceivable intervals of generation = $[-\Delta - \sigma^-, -\Delta + \gamma + \sigma^+]$ and release = $[\delta' - \sigma^-, \delta' + \sigma^+]$ (with $\delta' = \max(\delta, -\Delta + \gamma)$), are relative to `timeStamp`.

Table 14. Examples of unacceptable timing parametrizations

#	π	Δ	γ	δ	σ^-	σ^+	Recomm. R1 R2 R3 R4	Conceivable intervals Generation	Release	Slack (η)	Accuracy (α)
8	60	5	3	1	2	1	Y N Y Y	$[-7,-1]$	$[-1,2]$	3	2
9	60	11	3	5	8	5	N N Y Y	$[-19,-3]$	$[-3,10]$	8	10
10	60	10	5	14	3	3	Y Y N Y	$[-13,-2]$	$[11,17]$	7	17
11	60	55	5	10	8	2	N Y Y N	$[-63,-48]$	$[2,12]$	48	42
12	60	57	2	12	3	3	Y Y N N	$[-60,-52]$	$[9,15]$	54	52

Legend from Table 13 applies.